The official manual of the
Association of British Riding Schools

THE HORSE RIDER'S

HACKING HANDBOOK

The official manual of the
Association of British Riding Schools

THE HORSE RIDER'S

HACKING HANDBOOK

Karen Bush & Stephen Jenkinson

The Crowood Press

First published in 2011 by
The Crowood Press Ltd
Ramsbury, Marlborough
Wiltshire SN8 2HR

www.crowood.com

British Library Cataloguing-in-Publication Data
A catalogue record for this book is available from the British Library.

ISBN 978 1 84797 285 9

Illustrations by Claire Colvin.
Frontispiece courtesy RAD Photographic.

Typeset by Jean Cussons Typesetting, Diss, Norfolk
Printed and bound in Singapore by Craft Print International

Contents

Dedication

For Snip, Frosty, Shadow, Beauty, Copper, Tinkerbell, Hannah, Ninevah, Ben, Torosay, Simon, Shana, Hodl, 7Up, Miss Tweed, Minstrel, Hubble, Postie, Flash and all the other horses and ponies who have been responsible for so many memorable rides.

Karen Bush

For Jackie Delaney and Margaret Kent for their encouragement, Hamish and Polly for being such fun and honest horses, Lorna Mackay at Torrisdale Trekking and Cath Wrigley at Murthwaite Green for the best beach rides – ever! And to Jess for her ever-wagging tail when I return home.

Stephen Jenkinson

Acknowledgements

Thanks are due to Bob Atkins, Claire Colvin, Tina Constance, Kate Curry, Briony Dickins at RAD Photographic (www.RADFoto.co.uk), Sarah Fisher, Jackie Forster, Helen Foulis (Orkney Riding Club), Amy Gant, Lesley Gant, Anne Gray (Scottish Rural Property and Business Association), Peg Greiwe (Back Country Horsemen of America), Tony Hart (Australian Trail Horse Riders' Association), Heather Hoffman (BHS Ireland Participation Officer), Robyn Hood, Abi Mansley, Julian Marczak FABRS (ABRS), Nicky Moffatt at Horse and Rider, Corinne Moore, Shirley Renowden FABRS (ABRS), Libby Virgoe (Libby's Horse Tack), Lt Col K. G. Wesley FABRS (ABRS), Mark Weston and Sheila Hardy (BHS Kenilworth).

Foreword

by Julian Marczak, FABRS

There was once a time, not so very long ago, when riding in an enclosed arena was the exception rather than the rule, and one was fortunate indeed to be able to ride in a covered school protected from inclement weather. While such facilities have, of course, led to a major advance in 'all weather' riding, they have contributed generally to many riders, especially novices, becoming less experienced and capable of hacking out over varying terrain. Yet riding out, apart from the pleasure that can be gained by horse and rider, is something we owe to our horses wherever possible for their psychological well-being. This is aside from hacking for fittening, a break from schooling and returning to work after injury.

In *The Horse Rider's Hacking Handbook* Karen Bush and Stephen Jenkinson have covered every aspect of hacking in a highly professional and most comprehensive way, stressing throughout the essential safety considerations of the subject. It is a book containing a substantial amount of valuable information and guidance which will be invaluable to teachers, their pupils, leisure riders and, indeed, anyone wishing to hack out with their horse. The contents of the book, while written in some considerable depth, are presented in a highly structured and readable style making the publication a valuable reference manual.

The authors, through their high level of knowledge and experience, have produced clearly and concisely an excellent record of essential knowledge, and I have no doubt that *The Horse Rider's Hacking Handbook* will quickly become a key publication within the equestrian library.

Julian Marczak FABRS

(Julian Marczak is currently Chairman of the ABRS, and proprietor of Kings Barn Equestrian in West Sussex. Prior to this he was co-proprietor and chief instructor of the internationally renowned Suzanne's Riding School in Harrow, Middlesex, and Examinations Chairman of the ABRS. He is a Fellow of the ABRS and holds the highest qualification of the Association, the ABRS Principals Diploma, and is co-author of *The Principles of Teaching Riding* and *101 Riding Exercises*.)

Introduction

Most riders hack out at some point during their lives. For some of you it's a means to an end, helping to get your horse fit for competition and adding variety to the work schedule. It may also play a part in a rehabilitation programme following recovery from injury, or in rounding out the education of a young horse. But the majority of riders hack out purely for pleasure, and taking to lanes and bridleways can be a wonderful way for both you and your horse to relax and enjoy each other's company.

Our own hacking experience includes being clients at riding centres and guests on riding holidays, and on the other side of the coin, employment as ride escort for all ages and levels. We've hacked out on our own horses and on borrowed ones – some well behaved, others less so, and a few downright scary – and have been lucky enough to ride over a wide variety of terrain, from town centres to the edges of Scotland. On the whole it's been fun, which is just as it should be. Hacking should never be a chore, or boring, or frightening, or simply irritating because of some annoying habit your horse has, such as jogging. It should be a pleasurable and rewarding activity for you both – and just as importantly, it should also be safe.

Whether you have your own horse or hack out from a riding centre, are a serious or pleasure rider, novice or more advanced, this book has been written to help you solve any niggles and to get the most out of your hacking, whatever your level or ambitions. Notes for ride escorts have also been included where appropriate, but clients may also find these helpful in understanding what standards and procedures to expect when attending a riding school or equestrian holiday centre.

Happy hacking!

A NOTE ABOUT TTEAM

Throughout this book you will come across references to TTEAM and details of several TTEAM exercises you may find helpful. TTEAM is an acronym for Tellington-Touch Equine Awareness Method, a system devised by Linda Tellington-Jones over thirty years ago, and which evolved from her classical background with horses. The system of bodywork, groundwork and riding exercises can help reduce unwanted behaviours as well as improve performances.

I was initially sceptical about TTEAM, but a meeting with practitioner Sarah Fisher fifteen years ago changed my mind. Since then TTEAM has become one of my most valuable and versatile teaching 'tools'. It is a positive, humane and highly effective method which works without the need for fear, force or confrontation; in addition it teaches handlers and riders keen observation, and develops empathy and communication.

Horses that do TTEAM exercises show a marked improvement in their willingness and ability to learn and to cope with more challenging situations, which will obviously stand you in good stead out hacking or whenever trying anything new together.

Karen Bush

1 Getting Ready to Go

For most leisure riders, riding schools and holiday centres are the main sources of opportunity to ride out. Sometimes for regular groups of clients hacks and lessons are alternated with each other, or you may be able to book specifically for hacks only.

Joining a hack at a riding school or centre can also be a way for horse owners to enjoy riding in new surroundings, but without the hassle of having to transport your horse there – and as your escort will know the local area you won't need to research routes in advance. If you go away for a long weekend or holiday, it can also be a way of including some riding as part of your break.

FINDING A YARD

Before booking a ride, check out the centre first. You should look for:

- A tidy, well kept yard
- Well cared for horses
- Competent, courteous and friendly staff
- A current licence on display in the office area
- Association of British Riding Schools (ABRS) and/or British Horse Society (BHS) Approval: these help ensure a reputable establishment that meets high standards of safety and equine welfare

The ABRS and BHS websites both have databases to help you locate a school or centre. Many of these have their own websites so you can find out more about the establishment if it's too far away to visit in person beforehand.

Making a Booking

Book in plenty of time, especially if you want to ride during the busiest times, usually weekends. Arrive early if this is your first time, so you can fill out a rider registration form and be fitted with a hat if you need to hire one (*see* Chapter 2, page 25, The Hard Hat).

LICENCES

In the UK, anyone letting out horses for hire or for providing riding instruction is required by law to hold a riding establishment licence issued by the local authority. These are renewable annually and subject to compliance with licence conditions and a successful veterinary inspection plus payment of the licence fee.

In England, Scotland and Wales it is a condition of the licence that horses may not be let out on hire for riding or used for riding instruction without the supervision of a responsible person aged sixteen years or over. The only exception is in the case of horses let out for hire if the holder of the licence is satisfied that the hirer is competent to do so without supervision.

When making a telephone booking, you may be asked your height and weight so a suitable mount can be allocated to you. When you arrive, you may be weighed again as many people judge their weight incorrectly and don't take into account the extra weight of boots, hat and riding clothes.

Unless you are a regular or well known client, beware of any yard that doesn't enquire about your previous riding experience when making your booking. This helps staff to select the right horse for your ability, and decide on the most appropriate level of ride that you should join if riding in a group. Obviously, if you book a private hack for just yourself, or with a few friends, it can be tailored specifically to you, but expect to pay more for this facility.

Be honest about your ability and previous experience when booking a ride or holiday, and if you are nervous, have any anxieties, medical conditions or physical problems, make sure you tell the staff.

Medical Conditions

Along with contact details, you will be asked to list any medical conditions on your rider registration form. Complete this section fully and honestly: the information will be kept in confidence and is important for staff to know so they can take the appropriate action and inform emergency services in the event of you taking a fall. For the same reason, if riding out with a group of friends, tell at least one of them.

Being Assessed

If you have never ridden at the centre before, expect to be assessed before being allowed to hack out so they can be sure that you'll be able to cope. As an absolute minimum you should be able to mount, dismount and sit correctly, and to walk, turn the horse and halt. If you will

be trotting or cantering during the hack, you should be assessed at these gaits, too.

The procedure for an assessment varies: at some establishments you may be required to have a half-hour one-to-one lesson to determine your ability, after which you can make a booking to join a suitable level of hack. This may seem tiresome if you consider yourself a competent rider, but such policies are designed to ensure the safety and wellbeing of both you and the horse. If you will be going straight out on a ride immediately after your assessment – assuming you are considered capable enough – it also gives you a chance to familiarize yourself with the horse. If it's felt you would be better off partnered with a different horse, it is also much easier to make any changes at this point. If you have any concerns about him, now is the time to make them known.

If you've had a lengthy break out of the saddle, this assessment period is also the perfect opportunity to get back into the swing of things in a safe environment.

Riding holidays and days out which cater for complete beginners should give some basic instruction before you set out, for your comfort, confidence and safety, as well as the welfare of the horse. Be wary of any that don't, or that don't insist on wearing riding hats.

Riding Out

Most establishments will insist that you are accompanied by at least one adult escort. This is for the safety of you and the horse, and may be necessary to comply with insurance requirements. Some yards do offer unescorted horse hire, but check that you have adequate insurance cover, spend sufficient time accustoming yourself to the horse in a safe, enclosed area first, and follow the guidelines in the section Riding Alone (*see* Chapter 7, page 108) – or better still, go in the company of a friend.

NOTES FOR RIDE ESCORTS

- Clients should be mounted on a horse of an appropriate size and which is suitable in temperament and behaviour for the rider's ability.
- Escorting a ride, whether as leader or assistant, is not an excuse for exercising a young, inexperienced or excitable horse that will demand most of your attention and concentration and may be difficult to control in the event of an emergency (or even be the cause of one). Horses used as escorts must be steady and sensible enough that they can be used if necessary as a substitute for a client's horse. There should be no propensity to kick, spook or generally be difficult, and they should work equally happily at the front or rear of the ride, and stand quietly to be mounted and dismounted.
- Ride escorts should hold the BHS Riding & Road Safety Test (*see* Chapter 5, page 74) and be familiar with the Highway Code before escorting riders on the roads. This is also a prerequisite if you want to take any of the British Equestrian Tourism examinations.
- Ride escorts should be competent riders and handlers who either hold appropriate qualifications or have substantial practical experience.
- Greet all clients politely – your attitude can make all the difference, whether in attracting new clients or keeping the loyalty of old ones.
- Many health issues and disabilities are not obvious and do not affect a person's ability to ride, but the control of some conditions, such as epilepsy and diabetes, is not always perfect. Check rider registration forms so you know what action to take in the event of an incident. If you are unsure, discreetly ask the person before going out: be sensitive and tactful, and while you may keep a watchful eye on a person, don't obviously treat him or her as being especially fragile.

If you find you are unable to make a ride you have booked, ring to cancel as early as possible. Most establishments have a twenty-four-hour cancellation policy (sometimes longer) and you will be charged in full if your cancellation has not been made within this period.

FINDING A HORSE

If you prefer not to hire a horse from a yard, the options are to buy, share or loan. If you are planning to buy a horse you'll find plenty of information as to how to go about it and what to look for, not to mention being on the receiving end of plenty of well intentioned advice.

The best advice to take is that of your riding teacher, who will be familiar with your strengths and weaknesses, and will be honest with you about your abilities and the sort of horse to look for. When you find a horse you like, make a second appointment to visit it, this time with your teacher, to ensure that you are making the right decision.

Loaning or Sharing

An alternative to purchasing a horse may be to loan or share one. This will not be as responsibility free as hacking out from a riding centre, and is likely to involve financial commitment as well as willingness to help with chores, but on the plus side it enables you to form a closer bond with the horse you ride, and you may be able to enjoy more riding and with greater freedom. For a busy owner, a share arrangement can help with the horse's exercise, care and/or financial upkeep.

With a loan, the loanee usually takes on all the responsibilities and expenses associated with owning a horse but without the outlay involved in buying it. This can work well for an owner who may for various reasons (such as family or educational commitments) be unable to keep the horse in the short term, but is reluctant to sell it. For a loanee who may be able to meet running costs but doesn't currently have sufficient money to purchase, or younger riders who will outgrow a pony within a year or

so, it can also be a good arrangement; however, loaning and sharing have the potential to become a nightmare unless both parties vet each other very carefully.

Even good friends can fall out, so draw up a contract that covers all foreseeable eventualities in order to avoid future misunderstandings. If loaning or sharing your own horse, inform your insurance company, keep hold of any documents that prove ownership such as passport or breeding papers, and arrange to make regular visits. If loaning or sharing someone else's horse, check whether their insurance policy covers you; if not, make your own arrangements (*see* page 23, Insurance).

Before agreeing to any loan or share, make sure you are going to be compatible with the

Take time to get used to each other in a safe area at home before hacking out.

horse as well as with the owner. Find out how it behaves on and off roads, alone and in company; if you don't already know the horse, ask to actually see it out, accompanying it on foot or on a bicycle so you can observe it. Make sure you also ride it yourself (in a safe, enclosed area first) to ensure that you feel confident and in control.

Getting Used to Each Other

Having bought, or agreed to loan or share a horse, you may be keen to get out on some rides, but the roads are no place to start finding out about the quirks and foibles of a strange horse. Spend a little time getting used to each other first in a safe, enclosed area. You are as much an unknown quantity to him as he is to you: he may be more finely tuned than a riding school or trekking horse, and not used to being ridden by anyone other than his owner. When you do feel ready to go out for your first rides together, preferably go with another rider.

FIT FOR PURPOSE

Your horse doesn't need to be super fit if all you want to do is gently potter around together, but if he does nothing at all during the week other than being turned out in the field, it's unfair to expect him to go out for a whole day at the weekend, or to cope with faster rides. He will be liable to injury and even permanent damage, and will be stiff and sore afterwards, so be considerate and prepared to take things more gently.

Fitness Work

If you want to take part in a specific event such as a sponsored or long distance ride, or to take

him on a riding holiday, you may need to increase your horse's fitness levels.

The basic fittening programme outlined below assumes you will be riding five or six days a week, are starting from scratch, and aim to get your horse fit enough to take part in a 32km (20 mile) pleasure ride. If your horse is already semi-fit start off at the point you feel he's at – or if not aiming that high, simply adapt it to suit what you want to do. Allow extra time if he is being got fit for the first time, and remember that unforeseeable setbacks or minor injuries may delay progress. All horses are individuals and a fittening plan that suits one may not be right for another – so be observant, be adaptable, and use your common sense.

Basic Fittening Programme

Week 1: Ensure that the horse's feet and teeth are in good condition, and that vaccinations and worming are up to date. Build up from 15 to 20 minutes walking on the first day to 45 minutes by the end of the week. Work on level surfaces – if available, off road on good going is preferable and safer. Encourage an active walk. Keep an eye out for signs of sores or galling from saddlery.

Week 2: As for Week 1, walking actively for 1 hour.

Week 3: As for Week 2, building up to 1¼ hours.

Week 4: Hacking out up to 1¼ hours. Introduce slow and steady trotting on level, good going for approximately 2 to 3 minutes each time, building up to 10 minutes in total. Start to include some short schooling sessions.

Week 5: Hacking out up to 1¼ hours. Gradually increase the time spent in trot to a total of 20 minutes. Introduce hill work if possible. If all is going well, try a short canter towards the end of the week on known going, and preferably in a safe, enclosed area in case the horse becomes excited.

Week 6: Hacking out up to 1¼ hours. Increase the trot work to 25 minutes in total, and build up the canter work, avoiding hard or deep going to reduce the risk of concussion or strain.

Week 7: As Week 6.

Weeks 8–10: Hacking out for 1½ hours: steady work at all three gaits over varied terrain, trotting for up to 45 minutes in total. During Week 8 include a longer ride of around 2½ hours, aiming to cover around 25km (15½ miles) in this time. If the horse finds it a struggle, postpone doing the event and seek advice from your vet and an experienced trainer.

GOLDEN RULES OF A FITNESS PLAN

- Increase work slowly, with the emphasis on slow work initially.
- Increase feed *after* increasing work, not in anticipation of it.
- All horses are individuals, so adjust any fitness plans to suit each.
- As your horse becomes fitter his body shape will change, which will affect saddle fit, so have it checked and adjusted as necessary.
- As your fitness plan progresses, the amount of exercise your horse can cope with should increase; if he seems to be struggling it may be due to too little work, insufficient food or possibly a health problem. If you are not sure, consult your vet.
- Be more considerate with older horses: studies indicate a reduced capacity for exercise once they reach twenty years.

Feeding for Fitness

Keep a close eye on your horse's figure: being overweight increases the risk of laminitis, puts a strain on his limbs, lungs and heart, and will limit what you can do with him. Many owners tend to overestimate workload, and feed in excess of requirements. Much research has been done on the subject over the last thirty years, and feeding can nowadays be a bewildering and technical matter, but the good news is that free advice is available if you're not sure what or how much to feed. Many feed manufacturers employ highly knowledgeable nutritionists who will be able to help you plan suitable menus for your horse if you ring the customer helpline.

Checking Recovery Rates

Checking your horse's recovery rate after exercise can help you gauge how his fitness is progressing. Do this by taking his pulse at the point where the artery crosses under the jawbone just in front of the cheek. Place the balls of the index and second finger over it, and applying a gentle pressure, count the pulses

The easiest place to check the pulse is beneath the jawbone just in front of the cheek.

over half a minute, and then double it to give the number of beats per minute (bpm). Be patient if you can't immediately feel the pulse, which is slower than in humans. Try moving the position of your fingers and make sure you aren't pressing too hard as this will block the blood flow.

At rest, the normal pulse should be between 36–42bpm (beats per minute); take it over a period of five days at the same time to find the average. Don't take it just before going for a ride or at feed time, as it may be higher due to excitement. As your horse gets fitter, you may find that the resting heart rate becomes lower. Take the pulse at two, five and ten minutes after work: the heart rate should have recovered to below 60bpm within ten to fifteen minutes of rest, and should have returned to normal within thirty minutes. If after ten to fifteen minutes the pulse has recovered to 42–52bpm the workload can be increased, but if it is 72bpm or higher, the horse has been worked too hard for its current level of fitness.

Respiratory Rate

It can also be useful to know your horse's normal resting respiratory rate. Abnormalities of pulse and breathing rates can be indicators of pain, illness or stress, so it's well worth practising how to monitor both.

Stand slightly to the side and rear of the horse and watch the movement of the flanks. Count either the inward or the outward movement – not both – over a period of a minute. A normal resting rate should be in the region of eight to sixteen breaths per minute.

Signs of an Unfit Horse

Indications that you are working your horse harder than his level of fitness can cope with include:

- Fatigue.
- Slowing down.
- Distress.
- Blowing excessively.
- Dry, dull coat.
- Tucked up.
- Loss of appetite/not drinking.
- Poor heart recovery rate.
- Soreness and stiffness.
- Sweat is often foamy, sticky and smelly.

Returning to Work

Seek veterinary advice before returning your horse to work following recovery from an injury or surgery, as it may be necessary to take your fittening programme more slowly, and with regular veterinary reassessment and quite possibly physiotherapy treatment.

Even the most laid back of horses can become excitable if injury has necessitated a period of box rest or limited turnout, so when the time comes to begin ridden work again it's best to do so in a safely enclosed area with level going. Once the horse is ready to start hacking out away from the yard, go in the company of a steady horse. Always monitor the limbs carefully following exercise, and if you have any concerns, consult your vet before resuming the exercise programme.

Maintaining Fitness

Work or family commitments, spells of bad weather or shorter daylight hours in winter may mean you can't always ride as often as you'd like. Horses are generally better at maintaining fitness levels than humans, and at such times a horsewalker, if you have access to one, is better than nothing to help keep him ticking over. Your horse should also spend as much time as possible out in the field. This will not make him fit – horses tend to mooch around rather than

NOTE FOR RIDE ESCORTS

School horses that have had a break from hacking over the winter months should be ridden several times by competent staff when they start going out again as they can often initially be full of high spirits.

stride out actively – but gentle movement is preferable to none, and is also better for him psychologically than being confined to a stable for long periods. Being outside also gives him the chance to get used to potentially spooky things such as low-flying jets or farm machinery in nearby fields.

You could also hire someone responsible and competent to exercise your horse when you are unable to, or if he is kept at a riding school, consider working or part livery if he is suitable for such work. Make sure work hours are agreed, and bear in mind that he may not always be available for you to ride when you want to. Another option is a share agreement (*see* page 11, Loaning or Sharing).

If you can only ride three days a week, try to spread them out if possible rather than riding on successive days.

RIDER FITNESS

If you are new to riding, you'll quickly discover that it's a much more physical activity than you perhaps imagined. However, possessing a reasonable level of fitness will make hacking out more enjoyable for you, as the less fit you are, the quicker you'll tire, and as this happens, your posture will start to deteriorate. This will affect your security, make you more of a burden for your horse to carry, and can in turn lead to him becoming unbalanced and likely to tire more quickly himself. Fatigue also leads to loss of

concentration – important at any time when you're in the saddle, and especially so when out of doors in an unpredictable environment.

Increasing your general fitness levels won't just benefit your riding: you're also likely to feel fewer aches and pains afterwards, and if planning on going on a riding holiday, you should definitely consider it. Any extra activity you can fit into your daily routine will help – walk instead of driving or catching the bus, take the stairs instead of the lift – but if you're unaccustomed to taking much exercise, ask your doctor to check you out first, and start off gently.

If activities such as walking and jogging don't appeal, try things you find more fun, such as cycling, rollerblading, trampolining, swimming, or even line dancing, as you'll be more likely to keep them up. If you exercise at a gym, ask a trainer for advice on increasing suppleness and flexibility as well as cardiovascular fitness. Using equipment to improve muscle tone can be helpful, but avoid building muscle mass which will interfere with your position in the saddle.

Correct posture is such a key element in all spheres of riding, including hacking, that modalities such as Pilates and Alexander Technique are very helpful. There are also plenty of exercises which will increase general suppleness that you can try even while sitting at a desk at work, or when watching television in the evening; your riding teacher should be able to advise you on these.

HACKING NERVES

Nerves can be as much of a problem for those who hack as for competition riders. Sometimes there's a very good reason for it, but it's not always easy to put a finger on the source of your anxiety. Adults returning to the saddle after a long break often find themselves baffled to discover that their previous confidence seems to have deserted them, while those who are competent and confident within the enclosed environment of a covered school, can find themselves beset by anxiety on leaving its confines. Furthermore as you get older your sense of self-preservation often increases, making you less inclined to take even relatively minor physical risks, while reduced suppleness and stiffer joints affecting comfort, mobility and security can also sap confidence. But it needn't spoil your fun: simply adapt your approach to suit your needs.

Confidence crises are more common than you may think, and nothing to be ashamed of or embarrassed about. They are a normal physical and emotional response stemming from ancient survival traits – but they can be very powerful, and you may need help in learning how to overcome and control these instincts.

Discussing your worries with your riding teacher or ride escort may be enough to help you rationalize and solve the problem, but if nerves persist, many riders have found neuro linguistic programming (NLP) of help. NLP analyses the reasons why you may be nervous, and seeks to replace negative thoughts and feelings with positive ones.

In addition you are advised to observe the following:

- Don't ride out alone: taking someone with you, whether on foot, on a bicycle or on a steady horse, can help you feel more confident. Choose a companion who is calm, sensible and sympathetic to your problem.
- If you are apprehensive about riding the horse allocated to you at a riding centre, explain to staff that you are nervous and ask for a different one.
- If your anxiety stems from your horse's behaviour, get him checked over by your vet, and also by a saddler to ensure that this isn't caused by physical problems. (*See also* Chapter 8, page 134, Safety First).

- If you don't feel happy about taking certain routes, avoid them.
- Don't challenge yourself to tackle things you don't feel ready for!
- Never try a drop of 'Dutch courage' – alcohol can make nerves worse and adversely affect balance, co-ordination and judgement.

Ways of Reducing Nervousness

There are plenty of strategies that can help reduce anxieties; experiment to find which helps you most.

Activity: Vigorous physical activity such as walking briskly or sweeping the yard before riding may help remove stress chemicals in your system.

Improve your position: A correct position is also a secure one, so working on this can increase your confidence. A well schooled horse is also safer, more comfortable and obedient, so having regular lessons will benefit you both.

Breathing: Your breathing is often affected when you are stressed, becoming shallow, rapid or irregular. This raises stress levels even higher, and creates tension within your body, which will be communicated to your horse. Practising the breathing exercise explained below will help you to release tension and relax.

Breathing Exercise

Practise this exercise first while dismounted so there are no distractions, then use it at any time you begin to feel anxious.

- Either sitting or standing, place one hand on your abdomen: this will help you to think about breathing more deeply (keep both hands on the reins when you are riding)

- Breathe in deeply, slowly and steadily through your nose, noting how your hand is moved outwards.
- Hold your breath for a count of five, but without pressing your lips tightly together: keep them slightly parted so your jaw stays relaxed.
- Don't exhale abruptly, but breathe out in a controlled, slow and steady way, through slightly parted lips.
- Repeat.

Nervous Horses

Horses, as well as riders, can be affected by nerves (*see also* Chapter 8, pages 153–4, Napping, and 159–61, Shying and Spooking). An anxious rider can make a horse jittery – as prey animals they are very sensitive to body language indicating tension and fear – or the horse may simply lack in confidence. The combination of a nervous horse and anxious rider is to be avoided at all costs, as each will keep raising the stress levels of the other.

Developing or rebuilding confidence can take time, patience, knowledge, excellent observation and good riding skills. The suggestions offered here can help reduce stress levels while working through various confidence-building exercises (*see* Chapter 5, page 87, Confidence Training), but it is sensible in such situations to get help from an experienced trainer/practitioner initially.

A steady, sensible escort horse may act as a reassuring influence for some, but not all, and a horse that lacks confidence may be unsafe to ride out along roads. Remember that you have a responsibility not just for the safety of yourself and your horse, but for that of other road users too.

Ideas for You and Your Horse

Ride in the school or an enclosed area

before going out: This will enable you to settle your horse while simultaneously settling into the saddle yourself.

Flower essence remedies: Flower remedies help restore emotional balance – Bach Flower Rescue remedy is probably the one that most people are familiar with. Many people find it helpful in steadying the nerves when added to water and sipped at as required; alternatively it can be rubbed on the pulse points. It is also available as a spray that can be squirted directly into the mouth. Rescue remedy can be used safely by anyone, without danger of overdosing; it can also be used on your horse, applying it directly to his gums, tongue, or rubbing on his muzzle.

Aromatherapy oils: These highly concentrated extracts from natural plant products can have a rapid effect physically and emotionally. Inhalation is a quick and easy way to absorb them into the body, so you could try putting two or three drops on a tissue which you can keep in a pocket, ready to sniff at whenever you feel the need. Helpful oils include:

- Lavender – relaxing and calming in stressful situations.
- Pine – when nerves are due to lack of confidence.
- Geranium – reduces feelings of apprehension.
- Basil – counters feelings of negativity.

Buy good quality oils, and never apply them undiluted to your skin. If you are pregnant, suffer from epilepsy or high blood pressure, or are already taking medication, first consult your doctor or a qualified aromatherapist.

Aromatherapy oils can also be used to help anxious horses, but are used through a process of self-selection. Bearing this in mind, plus the fact that there are a huge number of oils, it is usually most practical and successful to consult an animal aromatherapist if you wish to try these with your horse.

Body wraps: TTEAM (*see* Introduction, page 8) body wraps may look odd, but can aid in developing a more correct and relaxed posture as well as decreasing feelings of anxiety. Elasticated tail or exercise bandages make ideal wraps, provided they still have plenty of stretch left in them. They need to be put on snugly enough to maintain a constant light sensation of contact with your body and not fall off or slip down, but not so tightly that they restrict or support your movement. They can also be used on your horse (*see* Chapter 8, page 158).

Try both these ways of putting on a wrap, as variations in placement can produce different responses.

Exercises to Try

Ear work and acupressure can also have a soothing effect. Perform the ear work exercise slowly, otherwise it will have an exciting rather than a calming influence. Adrenalin causes the nervous system to do things at great speed, so it may feel as though you are doing the work in a slow considered fashion when in fact you aren't. Take a deep breath before you start, and slowly let it out, consciously releasing any tension as you do so, and you'll find it easier to go slowly.

Ear Work

This TTEAM (*see* Introduction, page 8) exercise can be used to help calm you or your horse. In traditional Chinese medicine the triple heater meridian wraps round the base of the ear and affects the digestive, respiratory and reproductive systems. Ear work can therefore be a good way of dealing with the elevated breathing and tight feeling in your stomach which nerves can cause.

For you:
- Use a thumb and gently curled forefinger to stroke your ear, working from the inner to the outer edges.
- Move the position of finger and thumb slightly each time, so you cover the whole of the ear: when you've finished one, work on the other, but don't try and do both at the same time.

For your horse:
- Stand to the front and one side of your horse, lightly supporting his head by resting your fingers on the bridle or headcollar noseband. Move your other hand slowly and quietly towards the ear closest to you. Gently fold the edges together, and stroke gently but firmly and steadily along its length from base to tip, allowing your

fingers to slide gently off as they reach the tip.

● When your horse is happy with you doing this, slide your thumb inside the ear, with the rest of the hand cupped around the outside. Once again, slide from base to tip, moving the position of your thumb and hand slightly each time so the whole area of his ear is covered by your strokes. Work on one ear at a time: when you have finished one, start on the other.

Acupressure

Acupoints can be used at times of anxiety. Place the tip of your thumb directly on the acupoint at an angle of 90 degrees, and keep it there for thirty to sixty seconds whilst applying a little gentle pressure.

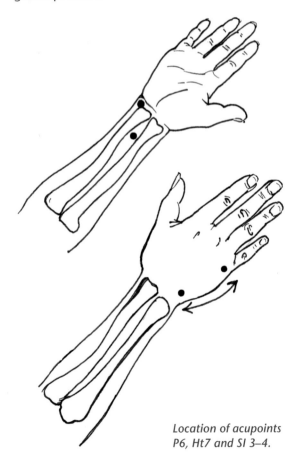

Location of acupoints P6, Ht7 and SI 3–4.

P6 (Inner Gate): Helps reduce fear. Located between the tendons on the underside of the wrist, approximately two-and-a-half finger widths back towards your body from the middle of the crease in your wrist.

NOTES FOR RIDE ESCORTS

● Don't be dismissive of a client's fears, even though they may seem incomprehensible and groundless to you: for your client they can be very real, and even disabling on occasion. Be sympathetic to their anxieties, and discuss ways in which they can be approached and solved. Would the client feel happier riding a different horse? Going for a ride on a one-to-one basis? Taken out on a lead rein? Would lessons to improve position help? Or even spending time getting to know the horse better by helping to groom and tack it up?

● Where a specific fear exists, explaining and demonstrating ways of coping with it may be helpful. Providing the knowledge and skills which might be needed to avert a situation arising (such as the horse bolting), as well as explaining what to do in the event of it happening, may help the rider cope with, and eventually overcome, their worries.

● Try wherever possible to focus on positive aspects rather than dwelling on 'what if' scenarios.

● Remember that it is your responsibility to ensure that the rider is appropriately mounted. If necessary change the horse if the rider is expressing anxiety or experiencing difficulty in maintaining control, and always remain within his or her ability.

Ht7 (Spirit's Gate): Helps to calm. Located on the little finger side of the wrist where there is a little groove between the ulna (main forearm bone) and the tendon.

SI 3–4: Reduces anxiety. Rub along the outer edge of your hand where the skin pattern changes, from the base of the small finger to the wrist crease.

> **NOTE FOR RIDE ESCORTS**
>
> New horses should be hacked out on at least several occasions by an experienced and competent member of staff to thoroughly assess them before they are used for clients.

INTRODUCING YOUNG HORSES TO HACKING

Never take a young horse out hacking until he understands and responds correctly to rein and leg aids – if he is still relying on voice aids, he isn't ready. Teaching the aids for moving the quarters over, and even to take a step back is also useful, and can help you keep him safe when on the roads.

While working on these at home you can also begin to prepare him for some of the things he'll encounter when out and about (*see* Chapter 5, page 87, Confidence Training). If he's had no acquaintance with traffic, spend time familiarizing him first with parked, and then moving cars: enlist the help of friends and family and do the same with motorbikes, bicycles, skateboards, baby buggies and anything else you may be likely to meet which you can feasibly set up. If stabled in a very quiet area, consider temporarily moving him to a busier environment where he can experience things such as traffic, farm machinery and low-flying jets whilst grazing or stabled near horses accustomed to, and unreactive to them.

Use an Escort Horse

Even though you may have spent a lot of time acquainting your youngster with various vehicles at home, they can be more challenging for him to cope with when he's off his home turf and they are moving faster and at closer quarters. Start on quiet roads, but try to avoid those which are really narrow as other road users will be forced to overtake more closely than on wider routes.

When you feel he's ready to go out, go with a confident person and a steady, sensible horse that will act as a good example to your youngster, and won't kick out or get upset should he bump him. Try not to let this happen, but make sure both are wearing protective boots, just in case. When riding in single file, the youngster should be positioned half to one horse's length from the escort, and kept nearer to the edge of the road, so that the escort horse helps shield him from traffic. When riding double, the youngster should be on the inside so the escort forms a barrier between you and any traffic. Ask vehicles and bikes to slow down or stop if necessary – if you need to keep both hands on the reins, let your escort give the hand signals.

After a few outings, if all is going well, allow the youngster to begin taking the lead: wait until the last hundred yards towards home, and rather than chasing him on, hold the escort back so the young horse begins to go on ahead and starts learning to be independent of his companion.

YOUNG RIDERS

As well as being a wonderful form of exercise for children, riding encourages social skills,

Riding and helping to care for ponies is a wonderful activity for children, but make sure they are supervised.

fosters respect for animals and humans, and develops confidence and responsibility. It is a high risk activity, however, so care needs to be taken to ensure the safety of the child. Basic safety precautions when handling and riding ponies should be taught right from the very first lesson, and adult supervision should continue for as long as it is felt necessary, however unwanted this may be by the child. As well as lacking in physical strength, co-ordination and stamina, children tend to lack foresight and the ability to judge speed and distance accurately, and they can be poor at maintaining concentration, and easily distracted.

There is no legal guideline as to the minimum age for leaving children unsupervised with a horse or pony, but it's suggested that this shouldn't be until at least twelve years old, the minimum age at which the BHS Riding & Road Safety Test can be taken (*see* Chapter 5, page 74). Passing the test is not a guarantee of sensible behaviour, however, so parents or guardians need to feel confident in the child's ability to ride responsibly with regard to safety and the welfare of their horse or pony. It is also advisable to insist that younger riders don't hack out alone, but go with a friend.

Saddlery

As much care should be taken to achieve correct fit and maintain the saddlery of children's horses and ponies as those of adults. Children can be slapdash, so the fit and condition of all items should be checked by a knowledgeable adult at least once weekly.

Saddle fit is often difficult with ponies due to their conformation: a common problem is that of the saddle slipping forwards. Ask a saddler to help find the best possible fit, and if the problem persists, fitting a point strap or using a crupper may resolve it. Cruppers need to be introduced very carefully as some ponies may dislike the feel; they also need to be kept scrupulously clean and supple, and the dock checked daily for any signs of chafing. It's important not to let the pony become overweight, as this makes saddles liable to slip sideways as well as forwards, in addition to leading to health issues.

Never allow a child to ride with their feet slipped through the loop above the irons, as they are likely to become trapped, which could prove fatal in the event of a fall. Punch extra holes in the stirrup leathers if they are too long.

Reins can also be dangerous if they are too long. As a temporary measure until your saddler can shorten them, tie a secure knot at the buckle end so the rider's feet don't become caught in the loop hanging down the pony's shoulder. Reins should also be a suitable width – what is comfortable for an adult can be too much of a handful for little fingers.

Legal Requirements

- In the UK it is a criminal offence to allow a child under the age of fourteen years to ride on the highway without correctly fastened protective headgear.
- Although insurance isn't compulsory, check that children are adequately covered: junior

NOTE FOR RIDE ESCORTS

Young children don't have the strength, stamina or concentration to cope with long periods of formal instruction, so going out for short rides on a leading rein can help keep riding a fun activity in this formative period.

rider policies for non-owners are available, often at a reduced premium.

INSURANCE

Unlike car drivers, insurance for horse riders is not obligatory, but it's certainly recommended, whether you ride regularly or only occasionally. Comparison websites can be helpful both in finding out what's available and narrowing down your choice, but ask other riders for personal recommendations, too. This will help you find out how easy an insurance provider has been to deal with, particularly in the event of making a claim. Online equine interest forums can also be good places to find out what other people have experienced.

Shop around for good deals, but bear in mind that the cheapest policy is not necessarily the best value. Don't just skim through brochures, but read policies carefully, especially the small print, and ring the company if there's anything you don't understand.

Horse insurance policies range from basic to very comprehensive, and can either be tailored to your specific requirements or bought as a package. When considering equine insurance, cover for veterinary bills probably springs to mind first, but Third Party and Personal Accident cover are equally important and should be included in your policy. Third Party cover will protect you from claims made against you by other people for which you are legally liable, including damage to property and injury. Personal Accident cover may only cover the owner of the horse, or it may cover anyone riding it with the owner's permission, and this is an important point to check if you loan or borrow a horse.

Although insurance isn't compulsory for private horse owners, it is for riding establishments in the UK, but you may want to take out a rider policy of your own anyway, and this will mean you will be covered if offered a ride on a friend's horse. For preference, choose a policy that includes Third Party cover and emergency veterinary treatment. Don't assume that other policies you hold, such as private health, accident, mortgage protection and life insurance cover you until you have checked, as horse riding may be classified as a dangerous sporting activity and excluded. If planning on riding abroad, check that travel insurance

covers you, and if you have a personal policy, that the cover extends to that country.

Most policies require that you take all reasonable precautions to prevent accidents and injuries. Most state that if you suffer a head injury and were not wearing protective headgear at the time you will not be covered. However, unless specifically stated in the policy – and read the small print very carefully – although failure to wear appropriate footwear or hi-vis garments may not invalidate your policy, it could in theory affect the benefits paid out if it was considered to be a contributory factor in the event of an accident or injury – particularly as you would be expected to follow the advisory notes on this in the Highway Code.

If you use a trailer or horsebox to travel your horse to different areas to hack out in, check your insurance policy to see if it offers cover for theft, and for recovery in the event of a breakdown. Not all vehicle recovery schemes are equipped to deal with horses.

2 Equipment

WHAT TO WEAR

Buying garments designed specifically for riding ensures comfort and freedom of movement, can minimize injuries and reduce the risk of accidents. With a huge range to choose from, you can be as stylish or conservative as you like.

If you are new to riding you may want to wait until you're sure this is an activity you're going to keep up before spending money on special clothes. Wear a pair of trousers, preferably without a heavy seam on the inside of the legs, as this can chafe: stretchy fabrics are also an advantage. Boots or shoes with closed toes, smooth soles and defined ½in (1.25cm) heels will be fine, although avoid those with large buckles or other decorative touches which could trap your feet in the stirrups.

A riding hat is the most important part of your dress, and no reputable riding establishment will let you ride without one: you can usually hire a hat, but check when booking your first ride. Once you decide riding is definitely for you, a hard hat of your own should be top of your shopping list, followed by specialist footwear.

The Hard Hat

A correctly fitted and secured hard hat is absolutely essential, and should be worn at all times while mounted. In the UK it is a legal requirement for children under the age of fourteen to wear one when on public highways, and in the US, several states have now also implemented similar legislation.

Always buy a new hat, rather than a second-hand one with an unknown history. Different brands may suit different head shapes, so a good fit can be affected by make as well as head circumference. In the UK, BETA (British Equestrian Trade Association) trained staff will be able to advise on the fit of any make or style of riding hat or helmet, whereas those trained by manufacturers may only be knowledgeable about their own products.

Riding hats and skull caps should conform to current safety standards. In the UK at the time of writing these are:

- EN 1384 – the basic minimum standard
- PAS 015
- Snell E2001

Look also for a BSI (British Standards Institute) kitemark label: this indicates that as well as conforming to the required standard, the hat continues to be subject to ongoing quality control checks.

A Damaged Hat

If your hat incurs severe impact – even just dropping it on a hard surface – although it may appear to be fine, there may be damage to the inner impact-absorbing layers that will compromise its ability to protect your head, and so it should be replaced.

Hat-fitting Tips

A correctly fitting hat should:

- Sit squarely on the head, just above the eyebrows and tops of the eyes.
- Be a close but not uncomfortably tight fit: it shouldn't rock forwards, backwards or side to side.
- Have a correctly adjusted retaining harness which should be fastened at all times while mounted.

The Body Protector

Designed to absorb impact from a fall or a kick from a horse, a body protector can be a sensible piece of additional clothing to wear when hacking out, especially if riding a young horse or planning to include some faster work or jumping during your ride.

Levels of protection vary: in the UK look for the highest, BETA Level 3 (purple label), and as with headgear, don't buy second-hand. A retailer with staff trained in fitting body protectors will help you find and adjust the style and size which best suits you. BETA advise replacing a body protector every three to five years, as impact-absorbing properties may decline with age and use; it is also important to replace it if dents are seen in it following a fall.

Footwear

Choose between short and long boots according to personal preference. Long boots look smart, but if close-fitting can be time-consuming to put on and take off. They do, however, provide good support for ankles and protection for your legs, and if you need to dismount to lead your horse through deep muddy going, the benefits are obvious.

Ankle-height boots are cooler in summer, although some riders prefer to use them all year round, often in combination with full or half chaps (*see below*).

There is a wide variety of types and styles to choose from, including trainers designed for riders if you prefer a casual look or want footwear suitable for other occasions. Unless using stirrups with toe cages, never wear ordinary trainers, or shoes or boots without a defined half-inch heel, as your feet could slip through the stirrup irons, resulting in loss of balance and being dragged in the event of a fall.

Don't wear Wellington boots either, unless they are designed specifically for riding in, as the heavy ridges and wide soles can make them liable to getting wedged in the irons.

Footwear should be comfortable to walk in as well as ride in, just in case you need to lead your horse home due to a problem.

Tops and Jackets

Wear garments appropriate to temperatures and weather conditions (*see* Chapter 6, page 91, Riding in Hot Weather, and page 99, Riding in Cold Weather). Choose tops with long sleeves which offer protection against grazes in the event of a fall, and against sunburn during the summer months.

- If you get too warm and want to remove a top or your jacket, always dismount to do so.

Jodhpurs and Riding Trousers

Jodhpurs or breeches are cut for comfort and ease of movement, but if you prefer the more informal look of jeans, buy a pair designed specifically for riding. These will incorporate all the features necessary to keep you comfortable in the saddle as well as doubling as casual wear.

The hoods of jackets or sweatshirts should be tucked inside – left hanging out like this they may get caught up on the branches of overhanging trees. Always fasten the front of a jacket too, so it can't flap and scare your horse. Poor position can also lead to accidents.

Normal denim jeans can lead to chafing and bruising, and may ride up the leg, bunching beneath the knees. If you are new to riding and only have jeans, choose a pair without heavy seams on the inner leg, which are fairly straight cut, and ideally are also stretch fabric.

Chaps

Worn over the top of jodhpurs, riding trousers or jeans, full-length chaps can reduce the chill factor considerably on cold breezy days. Some are also waterproof, but take care if made from fabrics which will be slippery to ride in, or that rustle and could scare your horse.

Half chaps worn with short ankle-length boots will help protect the legs from being pinched or bruised by the stirrup leathers. Many incorporate stretch panels, and are a useful alternative if you have large calf muscles and can't find full-length boots that fit. They can also be easier to put on and take off than full-length boots.

Gloves

Gloves increase your grip on the reins in wet weather, protect against cuts and grazes in the event of a fall, and help keep your hands warm in cold weather. Choose a pair that doesn't hinder your rein management, and in a light colour so hand signals are more obvious.

Eyewear

If you need to wear prescription spectacles, or want to wear sunglasses, the lenses should be shatterproof and the metal frames fitted with a padded bridge. Ask your optician to adjust the fit of the frames if necessary so they don't slip down your nose, and attach an elasticated sports band as well, just in case.

Contact lenses can make a big difference to safety and enjoyment when riding in rain, mist, or near the sea, but in dry conditions dust and dirt can irritate. If this happens remove the lens and wash out the eye as soon as possible.

● Tie long hair back so it doesn't get in your eyes or become entangled with anything.

Whip

If you want to carry a whip, take a short one, which will be less likely to get caught on anything, won't accidentally strike the horse of anyone riding next to you, and is easy to switch over into the other hand when necessary. It's usually most useful to carry it in the hand closest to the centre of the road, but if giving a signal with that hand, either swop it over, or hold the top of the handle with the thumb of the other hand.

What *Not* to Wear

Avoid wearing jewellery: bracelets, necklaces, dangly earrings and chunky rings can all cause nasty injuries if they get hooked up on anything. If you don't wish to remove a wedding ring, either wear gloves or cover it with a sticking plaster. If you need to wear a

---

NOTES FOR RIDE ESCORTS

● Dressing correctly and safely, and ensuring you are neat and tidy, is a mark of professionalism and of courtesy towards your clients: remember that you are also setting an example.
● Before setting off on a ride, take a minute or two while carrying out saddlery checks to ensure that your clients are correctly dressed. If you don't know them, this is also a good time to find out names and check on previous riding experience.

---

medi-alert tag, a close-fitting sports wristband-type is safer than a metal bracelet. If you need to wear a wristwatch, choose a leather or synthetic strap rather than a metal one, to minimize the risk of injury.

HI-VIS CLOTHING

Although you may be aware of the need to make yourself as conspicuous as possible during the winter months when dull days and bad weather can cause poor visibility, it's actually a policy you should adopt all year round.

The commonest reason given by motorists who have collided with a horse is 'I just didn't see it'. If you think this seems unlikely given the size of a horse, bear in mind that the majority tend to be bay, brown, black or chestnut – all colours which blend well with their backgrounds in both summer and winter.

Research shows that wearing hi-vis clothing can enable a motorist to see you around three seconds sooner than otherwise. This gives a driver travelling at 50mph (80km/h) an extra 72 yards (66m) of braking distance, and could make the difference between hitting you, and being able to slow sufficiently to drive safely around you.

Even when riding off the road, you should still wear hi-vis clothing, as it will make it easier for searchers to spot you should you fall from your horse and be knocked unconscious.

Fluorescent or Reflective?

During daylight hours fluorescent clothing is highly effective at increasing your visibility, but

Combine fluorescent and reflective fabrics for maximum visibility – notice how the blue jacket which has only reflective strips is less visible than the other one in daylight. (Courtesy RAD Photographic)

in dim or dull light conditions can appear dull. Reflective fabrics are better at such times as they shine in car headlights, reflecting up to 3,000 times more light back to the driver than white clothing. The best garments to choose are those which combine both fluorescent and reflective materials. As an absolute minimum, wear a tabard, but ideally wear more. There are plenty of hi-vis clothes and accessories for you and your horse, including the following:

Hat cover/band: This may be the first indication a motorist has of your presence ahead when driving along twisty roads edged by high hedges.

Jacket: A jacket gives a larger area of visibility than a tabard.

Leg bands: The constant movement helps catch a driver's attention, while the low position is picked up earlier by car headlights. Ideally, put leg bands on all four of your horse's legs, but if you have only two, place them on the foreleg and hind leg closest to the centre of the road. You can also buy leg bands for riders.

Exercise sheet or tail cover: A hi-vis sheet is especially effective as it covers a large area. Lightweight mesh as well as fleece-lined and waterproof versions are available to suit all weathers.

Nose/browband covers, neckbands and breastplates: These help catch the eye of oncoming drivers; rein covers are less helpful.

Gloves: Adding reflective and fluorescent patches to glove backs, or using hi-vis glove covers will help ensure clearly visible hand signals; armbands will also help with this.

Lighting Up

It's best to avoid being out as dusk falls or when it's dark: be aware that at certain times of year the light can fade very quickly, and plan your rides accordingly, allowing sufficient time to return home from your ride.

In the UK, the Highway Code advises that in addition to hi-vis clothing, a light showing red to the rear and white to the front is fitted to the rider's right arm and/or leg at times when visibility is poor. Safety lights and battery-operated LED lights can be purchased from equestrian retailers and cycling shops, available as flashing tabards, belts and tailguards as well as units that can be strapped to riding hats, arms, legs or stirrups.

- You can often find a wide range of competitively priced hi-vis clothing at suppliers specializing in personal protective equipment for outdoor workers.

SADDLERY

The Highway Code requires that you should ride with both a saddle and a bridle. Always check that all saddlery is safe and correctly fitted and adjusted before setting out. If you are riding someone else's horse or one from a riding or trekking establishment and spot a problem, point it out and politely but firmly insist on it being put right, rather than risk an accident.

NOTES FOR RIDE ESCORTS

All ride escorts should wear at least a hi-vis tabard at all times: they should also be worn by all clients when riding on the road. Keep spare tabards for clients who do not have their own.

Some horses may be more exuberant in behaviour out hacking than when working in a ménage or school, and a different bit or the addition of a martingale may be helpful. However, always try out any change of saddlery at home in a safe enclosed area first, so you know how your horse will respond. If his behaviour goes beyond simply being a little over-enthusiastic at the outset of a ride, using increasingly severe or restrictive items of saddlery is not necessarily the answer, and may even cause a worsening of the problem. Rather than dealing only with the symptoms, you should investigate and remedy any underlying cause(s), and avoid putting your horse in situations you know will create difficulties.

If you have difficulty in controlling your horse, you should question whether it is safe to ride out with him, especially if you will be on roads.

The Bridle

Bridles can cause much discomfort if they don't fit properly: browbands are a common problem area – if too small, the headpiece is pulled forwards into the base of the ears. On longer rides where you may want to remove your horse's bridle when taking a break, the type which doubles as a headcollar is handy. Webbing bridles provide an easy-care alternative to leather, especially if riding regularly on beaches or in heavy rain.

Bitless bridles are popular with many endurance riders, but are not for everyone: some horses go well in them and others don't. Riding skills need to be just as good as when using a bitted bridle – the bitless bridle is no excuse for poor hands. It is also a good idea to check with your insurance company to ensure you are covered whilst using one.

Reins

Reins come in different lengths and widths,

and it is important to choose a pair appropriate for the size of your hands as well as your horse or pony. If too narrow they will be difficult to hold, and if too wide can be an awkward handful. Rubber-covered or webbing reins are less slippery to hold than plain leather when wet from rain or sweat. Rubber-covered, laced or plaited leather reins are easier to keep hold of than plain leather when wet from rain or sweat, but can cause blisters on the fingers if you aren't wearing gloves; alternatively webbing reins, with or without grips stitched on, are durable and comfortable to hold.

The Saddle

After hundreds of years when there was little change in the basic design of saddles, the last three decades have seen huge advances. Nowadays you can choose from full trees, half trees or no trees, traditional leather or synthetic materials, and you can even get adjustable trees and inflatable panels – plus of course there is a whole range of specialist saddles available for every equestrian activity.

Whatever your preferred style, it's crucial that the saddle fits the horse otherwise it will cause discomfort, leading to incorrect gait movement, injury and behavioural problems. It must also fit the rider, if he or she is to be secure, balanced and comfortable – all factors that will influence the horse's own comfort and stability. Suitability is also important: if your preference is for the English style, then a general purpose (GP) or an endurance saddle is a better choice than for example a dressage saddle, which has a short, deep seat and straight-cut flaps that will limit how much you can move your seat and shorten your stirrups, making it difficult to adapt your position according to variations in terrain.

Your horse can change shape considerably between the winter and summer months, and also according to age, and how much and what sort of work he's doing, so saddle fit should be checked at least annually, but preferably every six months, and adjusted or changed as necessary.

Saddlecloths and Pads

Saddlecloths, pads and numnahs can help keep saddle linings clean, and some also have wicking and cushioning properties. Very thick ones may alter the fit of the saddle and make it narrower, so take care in your choice: they should also be pulled well up into the front arch of the saddle to avoid pressure on the withers. Check that any loops provided for girth straps do not pull the cloth back on to the withers.

Girths

Girths come in many shapes and styles, and you may need to experiment to find which best suits your horse. Those made of fibres with a degree of 'give' in them allow for ribcage expansion and greater comfort; this can also be achieved with elasticated inserts, in which case choose a girth with elastic at both ends as this creates better saddle stability.

When fully tightened, the girth buckles should reach about halfway up the girth straps on both sides; this stops them forming an uncomfortable lump under the top of the thighs and allows further room for adjustment if necessary. Once adjusted, pull the buckle guards down over the girth straps to protect the saddle flaps from damage. Some saddles are designed with extra long girth straps to be used with a short girth, which reduces bulk beneath the rider's thighs: take care, however, that the girth is the right length and the skin does not become nipped between it and the bottom of the saddle flap.

Stirrup Leathers

If the stirrup leathers don't have enough holes to shorten them sufficiently, make some more with a hole punch: don't twist the stirrup leathers round the irons to shorten them, as this damages them and causes the irons to hang at an awkward angle. As well as being uncomfortable, your feet could become wedged, which could cause you serious injury in the event of a fall. Also never push the feet through the loop of leather just above the irons, as this is equally risky.

Some riders prefer leathers which adjust near the stirrup iron, as these reduce bulk beneath the leg, allowing for a closer contact with the horse; however they need to be adjusted from the ground, and can be more of a fiddle.

Both leathers should always be adjusted so they are the same length, otherwise you will ride with your weight unevenly distributed across your horse's back, affecting his comfort and balance. Leathers made from leather can stretch unevenly, so swop them over once a week to try and keep them as equal as possible.

Stirrup Irons

If you have your own horse and can equip it as you wish, it's sensible to use a safety stirrup of some kind. There's a wide variety available, but whichever style you choose, make sure they are suitable for your weight. It is also vital that whatever the type of stirrup, they are wide enough for your feet so there is no risk of them either slipping through or becoming wedged: there should be about ½in (0.75cm) of space between each side of your foot and the sides of the irons. Remember that changing your style of boot may change the amount of clearance at each side. If at a riding centre, always ask for different irons if they are too small or too large.

Heavier irons will tend to swing less and be easier to regain if you lose one. Adding rubber

STIRRUP LENGTH

The 'right' stirrup length depends on your level of experience (more advanced riders will generally ride longer than beginners and novices) and the activity you are engaged in. For hacking out it should be somewhere between your usual flatwork and jumping length, as this will make it easier for you to adopt a 'half' seat, which will help you stay in balance with your horse over varied terrain, deepen your heels if needed, and jump small obstacles and ditches; it allows the joints to work easily and comfortably as shock absorbers, and still gives you good control, use of the leg aids and security in the saddle.

As a general rule of thumb, you'll usually need to shorten your stirrup leathers between two and four holes from your flatwork length, depending on how long you normally ride.

If you need to adjust the length of your stirrup leathers while mounted, keep your foot in the stirrup as you do so. This makes it easier to find the right length, and is safer if anything unexpected happens and you quickly need to regain control. With the reins in one hand, use the other to pull the buckle out away from the saddle and shorten or lengthen the leather as appropriate: use more or less pressure from your foot on the stirrup to help you do so. Once the stirrup is the right length, pull the buckle back up so it lies close against the stirrup bar and cover it with the saddle's skirt so it doesn't bruise your thigh.

You can roughly estimate the length of stirrup before mounting by placing one hand on the stirrup bar and measuring the leather along your arm – the iron should just reach your armpit.

If you need to adjust the length of the stirrup leathers while mounted, keep your foot in the stirrup as you do so. This is safer if anything unexpected happens and you need to regain control.

treads will stop the feet slipping around in the irons, reducing the likelihood of this happening, but if it does, raise your toe a little and turn it inwards to find the stirrup iron again. It is worth practising this at home so you become proficient at it.

Accessories

Breastplate: This can be helpful if riding in hilly areas as it helps prevent any risk of the saddle slipping back.

Saddlebags: These range from small, relatively cheap saddlebags and drink coolers which will hold a drink, sandwich and a few other essentials, to more capacious panniers. If they are not waterproof, put anything you want to keep dry inside a plastic bag. Load them evenly, and make sure they are fitted securely and won't bounce around. A fleece lining where they rest against your horse can help prevent chafing. Always try them out at home in a safe enclosed area, first allowing your horse to have a good look at them and to sniff them if he wishes before putting them on. Lead him in hand at walk and trot to assess his behaviour, and check whether they need to be adjusted more securely before mounting. Ride in walk, trot and canter to check they don't interfere with your position or shift around – they may be fine in walk but not so good when going faster.

Neckstrap: Essential if your horse has a hogged mane, and can still be handy as an emergency grab strap. If you use a stirrup leather, it will also mean you have a spare for emergencies.

Headcollar and leadrope: On longer rides this will enable you to tie up your horse at stops along the way. Fit a lightweight nylon headcollar beneath the bridle, or use a bridle that doubles as a headcollar.

Exercise rug/rainsheet: Your horse may need some protection against the elements in cold or wet weather; using a hi-vis one will also make you more visible. Make sure they are fitted with a fillet string which will prevent a gust of wind from blowing them up, which may spook your horse.

Protective boots: *See* page 35, Leg Protection.

Maintenance of Saddlery

Check all saddlery when cleaning it as well as when tacking up. Test for weak stitching by gently tugging at it, check for cracking in leather, buckles that are bent or have shortened, worn tongues, and look for places

NOTES FOR RIDE ESCORTS

- No matter how competent the clients are, always ensure that either you, or a competent member of staff, check each horse's saddlery for safety before leaving the yard.
- Teach all riders how to check and tighten the girth themselves while mounted. Check that all girths are tightened sufficiently before setting out on the ride.
- If re-checking girth tightness while out on a ride, choose a suitable, quiet place to do so, away from passing traffic. Ensure that safe distances are kept between each of the horses while this is going on, and keep an eye out for riders who may drop their reins, allowing their horse to wander.
- In the yard tackroom, keeping a range of different stirrup-iron sizes already threaded on to leathers will enable a quick changeover to be made if needed.

where buckle holes have run into each other. Other danger spots are thin, stretched and weak areas where leather comes into contact with metal, such as where reins and cheekpieces attach to the bit, or stirrup leathers to the irons. If anything is damaged or faulty, get it repaired or replaced, but don't risk using it.

Regular cleaning will prolong the life of saddlery and minimizes the likelihood of it chafing your horse's skin. Clean leather items using warm water, followed by a proprietary leather soap or conditioner to help nourish it and keep it supple. Saddlery made from synthetic materials is generally lower maintenance than leather but still needs regular checking and cleaning, following the manufacturer's instructions.

LEG PROTECTION

Horses with poor conformation, or lacking balance, experience or fitness, may need some kind of leg protection – and even if your horse is beautifully put together and has faultless action, you may decide it's a precaution you want to take anyway. Knocks, bumps and accidents can easily happen when riding over uneven terrain or if popping over any small obstacles you meet along the way, and even the most predictable road surface can sometimes prove treacherously slippery.

Boots are preferable to bandages – unless your vet has advised you to use bandages – as they're quicker, easier and safer to put on, and won't stretch and sag if they get wet, or tighten as they begin to dry out.

Brushing and Knee Boots

Brushing boots will give reasonable protection to the cannons and fetlock joints; when riding on tarmac or concrete roads, or on stony or gravelled tracks, you may like to add knee

boots too, as these surfaces can be very unforgiving and may inflict nasty injuries if your horse goes down on one or both knees. You can buy these separately, or brushing boots which incorporate knee protection are available.

Boots made from synthetic materials are usually easiest to care for, and come in a range of colours, including hi-vis. Look for breathable qualities, and avoid stitching that comes into direct contact with the legs, as this can lead to chafing. Velcro straps are popular as they are quick and easy to fasten and difficult to overtighten, but they need to be kept really clean or they won't stay done up: it can be a good idea to tape them over to ensure they stay in place, as a flapping or slipping boot may bring your horse down.

Overreach Boots

Overreach boots may be advisable if your horse is not very well balanced, but choose a type that won't flip up if you go through mud or water (both occasions when overreaching is more likely to happen), and won't trip him up if he stands on the back of one.

Problems with Boots

The down side of using boots is that the horse's legs can become sweaty, and there is always the risk of dirt and grit working its way between boot and leg, which can cause chafing; therefore on longer rides you'll need to weigh up their advantages and disadvantages when deciding whether to use them. Always check very carefully for any signs of soreness when removing them, and minimize the risk of it happening by ensuring the following:

- They are the right size for your horse.
- They are a snug, but not tight fit.

- Legs are clean before putting them on.
- Linings are cleaned thoroughly after use – never use dirty or sweaty boots.

COMFORT IN THE SADDLE

The more time you spend in the saddle, the more important comfort becomes – even a short ride can seem like hours if something is hurting. A correct, well balanced position will be comfortable as well as secure and effective, but other things can contribute to, or detract from your enjoyment and interfere with your concentration.

Comfort for the Feet

Stirrups with extra wide treads and shock-absorbing properties give better support and weight distribution when riding for long periods; you can also buy gel insoles for your boots. Socks that slide down and end up balled into the toes of your boots can be very uncomfortable: look for elasticated grips round the top, ribbed arches, and a good fit.

Underpants

The most comfortable underwear may not look very attractive, but remember you are dressing for practicality and comfort, not fashion! Skimpy or lace-trimmed knickers can be a curse, and thongs are also best avoided. Many male riders possibly suffer needlessly due to poor underwear choice. Snug-fitting briefs are preferable to baggy boxers, but don't confuse supportive with a tight or restrictive fit. A general purpose athletic supporter can also help, as can specially designed equestrian support briefs for male riders – experiment to find the best option for your body.

Female Support

For ladies, a good bra is essential for comfort and health. Look for features such as wide shoulder straps, seamless or with seams on the outside, and fabrics with breathable and wicking properties. A wide band at the bottom can help prevent it from riding up, and if buying a sports bra, pick one that is rated for high impact. Those who are 'C' cup and above may find shaped cups better than vest-type bras, but avoid underwired bras, as wires can break free and pierce the armpit. The right size is vital if a bra is to do its job effectively – and as it is estimated that over 70 per cent of women wear the wrong bra size, it may be a good idea to get yourself properly fitted. A better fit is more likely if you look for a bra with a specific size rating rather than the more generalized small, medium or large fitting, but be prepared to try different makes and shapes until you find the one that best suits you personally.

The Saddle

The saddle needs to fit you just as well as the horse, because if it is too wide, too narrow or too short you'll be uncomfortable; however, it is usually possible to find something that suits you both. Riders of slighter build and who lack in natural padding may find padded underpants a help; these are available from many equestrian retailers, or alternatively try padded cycle shorts under your jodhpurs. Seat savers made from gel, foam, sheepskin or synthetic sheepskin can be another solution.

Clothes

When buying riding clothes, choose garments which fit you *now*, not the size you hope you'll be when you've finished your diet in six months

Don't wait until your horse needs shoeing, but make a regular appointment with the farrier.

time! Allow extra room if you plan to wear a body protector under a garment such as a jacket. Dress according to the weather (*see* Chapter 6, page 91, Riding in Hot Weather, and page 99, Riding in Cold Weather).

HOOF CARE

Horseshoes help to prevent excessive wear on the hooves from hard surfaces, which will make your horse footsore. As the feet grow constantly, regular re-shoeing will be necessary, with the frequency varying between individuals depending on genetic as well as

environmental and nutritional factors. Usually the timescale is between four to six weeks: leaving it longer and letting the hoof get overlong can lead to physical injuries such as strains, and will predispose the horse to stumbling and losing shoes.

Check the feet at least once each day, and always before and after a ride. Pick them out working from heels to toe, removing any packed mud and stones, and inspecting the condition of each shoe. This is also the perfect opportunity to run your hands down your horse's legs looking for any lumps, bumps or cuts. The following signs indicate that your horse is in need of re-shoeing:

- Long feet.
- Hoof growing over the edge of the shoes.
- Risen clenches.
- Very worn or distorted shoe.
- Lost shoe.
- Loose shoe – sometimes you will hear a clanking noise as the horse moves on hard ground.

Risen clenches can cause a nasty injury if your horse brushes: use a hammer to tap them down again for the moment, and make an appointment with the farrier. Do not ride out if your horse has a loose shoe. Sometimes it may be necessary for you to remove a shoe, so keep a set of tools on hand and ask your farrier to show you how to do this (*see* Chapter 6, page 150, Lost Shoe).

Hoof Health

Well balanced feeding throughout the year is essential for healthy feet: if you need advice on your horse's diet, most feed manufacturers have helplines where you can obtain advice from equine nutritionists.

A wide range of hoof dressings is available: some may be beneficial to horn quality, but others are more for cosmetic purposes and may not be appropriate for your horse. Ask your farrier for advice and any recommendations as to the best products to use.

Going 'Barefoot'

Keeping your horse 'barefoot' or unshod is an option rapidly growing in popularity. A number of endurance horses currently compete successfully barefoot, and there can be some advantages.

- Unshod hooves tend to grip the ground well.

- Without the restriction of rigid shoes and nails, feet are better able to expand and act as shock absorbers.
- The frog is better able to fulfil its functions of shock absorption, blood circulation and aiding grip.
- Hooves will wear more naturally in the shape most comfortable to the horse.
- There is less risk of injury from kicks in the field.

Going barefoot isn't suitable for all horses, however, and can depend on factors such as hoof condition, conformation, management, build and weight, as well as the work you plan doing. If you can't avoid roadwork, hooves may be worn back faster than they can grow, and barefoot might not be a realistic choice.

Whether going barefoot is a possibility for your horse or not will need to be assessed by your farrier. Even if your horse isn't the ideal candidate, it may be possible to compromise by shoeing in front only, as the front feet tend to wear more quickly.

If you decide to try it, it will take time for the feet to toughen up and you will have to build up work slowly and gradually. The feet will still need trimming every eight weeks or so to help keep them in good shape. They may be more susceptible to bruising and punctures than shod feet, and if the ground is baked hard by the summer sun it can be as unforgiving as tarmac surfaces: however, hoof boots can offer protection when the terrain is more demanding.

Hoof Boots

Hoof boots can be useful for horses making the transition to going barefoot, as well as for those who already have, but need foot protection on more rugged surfaces to which they are not accustomed. A spare boot can also be handy for shod horses: if you lose a shoe it will help prevent further damage to the foot.

Some boots are more durable than others – in some cases they can outlast steel shoes by 3:1, but it depends on the terrain the horse is working on, his movement and conformation, as well as the amount of use they get.

A number of different boots are available; some are only suitable for light hacking, so buy a style appropriate for your activities. It is also essential that they are the best possible fit otherwise they may chafe or be shucked off, so read the manufacturer's sizing guides carefully. You may also need to select two different makes of boot, as front feet are generally rounder in shape than back ones, and you will need to choose the boot which best conforms to this.

Feet should be booted in pairs – both front feet and/or both back feet, never singly (unless you are using one to protect a hoof that has lost a shoe). They should not be left on for more than twelve hours, or according to the manufacturer's recommendations: most are suitable for rides of up to 25 miles (40km). Using them for longer periods may be possible, but accessories may be needed in order to do so safely and comfortably – check the manufacturer's guidelines.

● Make sure you know how to put a boot on before you actually need to use it in an emergency.

WHAT TO TAKE WITH YOU

Even if you're only going out on a short, well known route, be prepared for the unexpected – accidents can happen just as easily close to home as when you're many miles away. It is suggested that you always take the following items:

Mobile (cell) phone: Make sure the battery is fully charged, and that essential numbers you may need are entered on the address book function (*see also* Chapter 8, page 133, Emergencies). Either set it to silent mode or switch it off (which will also preserve battery power) while you're riding to ensure you aren't distracted or your horse startled should someone ring.

Phone card and change: Mobile phones aren't infallible, and can become damaged or lose the signal, so have a phone card and change as back-up in case you need to use a public payphone.

Rider ID: Include your name, address and contact details for next of kin or other person to contact in an emergency, your GP, vet and the yard where your horse is stabled, plus any medical information. Laminate the paper or card to make it more durable, and place it inside a pocket – not inside your hat, where it may not be discovered until much later.

Horse ID: In case you part company with your horse and he runs off, make sure there's some kind of ID on him, such as engraved discs attached to both the bridle and saddle. Leather luggage labels fixed to a saddle D ring can also work well and can contain lots of information. Ensure your contact information is included, plus the vet's number in case he's injured when found.

Hoofpick: The folding type will fit in a pocket or can be tied to a saddle D-ring.

Pocket first aid kit: Small basic kits can be bought from saddlers or chemists in neat packs that can be slipped into a pocket, or you could make up your own.

● Carry all essential emergency equipment such as first aid kit, whistle and mobile phone on yourself, so you have it to hand if you part company with your horse and he runs off.

Additional Equipment

When going out on longer rides or in more isolated areas it is also helpful to take the following items of equipment:

Headcollar: Put this on under the bridle if you are likely to want to tie your horse up. This will avoid making awkward changeovers and the risk of your horse getting loose: choose a lightweight one which won't be too bulky and will fit comfortably beneath the bridle. Alternatively, buy a dual-purpose web bridle that converts into a headcollar by unclipping the bit from each side.

Leadrope: Clip one end of the leadrope to the headcollar ring beneath the jaw, loop the other end round the neck, and tie it with a non-slip knot such as a bowline. Alternatively, coil the rope neatly and clip it on to a saddle D-ring.

Baler twine: Useful for tying up awkward gates if necessary.

Piece of string: Lightweight and breakable, in case you need to tie your horse up. You can also buy rubber safety ties that do the same job, but never tie your horse directly to a fixed object: should he pull back for some reason and find his movements limited he may panic and could seriously injure himself in his struggle to free himself.

> **NOTE FOR RIDE ESCORTS**
>
> No matter how short a ride may be, always carry a first aid kit, a lead rein, a mobile phone and money/phonecards for a public payphone. Know the location of public payphones along the route, or of houses, shops or other places where an emergency call can be made in areas where the mobile signal may be weak. Check that any clients who are carrying mobile phones have switched them off before you set out. Ensure there is someone at the yard you can contact at any time if you need help or recovery.

Whistle: If you need to attract attention, the noise will carry better than your voice, and it is less tiring to blow a whistle than to be constantly shouting.

Horseman's penknife: These specially designed pocket tools contain a number of useful gadgets that can come in handy in all sorts of situations.

Spare stirrup leather: Buckled around the neck, this will also double as a neckstrap to help you stay balanced and secure.

Map and compass: *See* pages 52–3, Finding your Way.

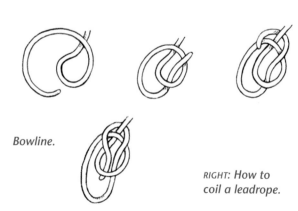

Bowline.

RIGHT: *How to coil a leadrope.*

3 Where to Ride

WHERE YOU CAN GO

When you first learn to ride or hack out, you will usually be riding with others, or following local routes that you've been shown. While it may not have been obvious, even on short rides you will probably have used different types of access rights and permissions. In some places you will have a right to ride there, in other places your presence may only be due to the landowners' benevolence; and in some cases, riding along a track may simply be a tradition that has only continued because no one has challenged it. The vast majority of land in Europe and the English-speaking world is owned by someone. So unless you only ride on your own land, you will almost always be hacking out on someone else's property.

You get the opportunity to ride on other people's land for two main reasons. Firstly, in many countries there are longstanding, legally protected rights and traditions that give a right of access across private land. The second reason is that if no right of access exists, landowners can still voluntarily allow people

Many long distance and recreational paths have their own special symbols as well as waymarks to help people keep to the specific route. (Courtesy RAD Photographic)

to ride over their land: this is termed 'permissive' or 'concessionary' access.

So as you start to explore further afield, it's important to know where you can ride in order to maximize your enjoyment and minimize problems for other people.

Signposting and Waymarks

Small directional arrows called 'waymarks' are often placed along routes on walls, gates, posts or trees, to help path users find their way and so avoid unintentional trespass. Many long distance and recreational paths have their own special symbols as well as waymarks to help people keep to the specific route.

In England and Wales local councils have a legal duty to indicate places where a public right of way leaves a surfaced road. This task is far from complete in many areas, so the lack of a signpost doesn't necessarily mean there's no right of way. Specific colours are used to waymark the different types of right of way for riders, such as blue for bridleway or red for byway. White is usually used on permissive paths irrespective of who the route is for.

These colours are also sometimes used on signposts, although some councils use silhouettes of walkers, horse riders and cyclists to show more clearly who has rights to be there; yellow arrows indicate public footpaths. Sometimes there are inconsistencies in the colours used: confusingly, some toll rides use the same colours as those used to denote public rights of way.

In Scotland, recent changes to the law have meant that walkers, horse riders and cyclists can all use most routes, and signposts are gradually being updated to show simply directions, destinations and distances; advisory information may be added if hazards or other natural restrictions are not obvious. However, until this changeover is complete, you may still find 'footpath' signs on some routes that can be responsibly ridden. Increasingly, you will only see 'no riding' signs on the rare occasions where there is a definite legal ban. The colours of any arrows generally differentiate between promoted trails, rather than who can use that route.

In Ireland, because of very limited access, the routes that do exist are often waymarked and signposted; many are permissive, and most are not for horse riders. As in Scotland, the colours of waymarks differentiate between different promoted routes, rather than access rights.

ACCESS RIGHTS IN ENGLAND AND WALES

Public Rights of Way

There are around 42,000 miles (67,600km) of officially recorded public rights of way for horse riders to use across England and Wales, and which form the heart of the off-road riding network. Some areas have an extensive local rights of way network, in others the network is fragmented and ill suited to the needs of recreational horse riders. Public rights of way (PROWs) are the most valuable type of access because in most cases:

● They have the highest level of legal protection.
● They can be used by the public at any time of day or night.
● It is a criminal offence to make them harder or more dangerous to use.
● Detailed records are kept by local councils.
● They are shown on Ordnance Survey maps.
● It is difficult to legally close or divert them.

The best way to find where they are is to look at an Ordnance Survey (OS) Explorer Map (*see* page 52, Maps). These maps cover the whole of England and Wales and use different green lines

Many bridleways are ancient routes established centuries ago when people used to go about their everyday lives on foot or on horseback. (Courtesy RAD Photographic)

to show the different public rights of way; these are described below.

Public footpaths: These are a legally protected right of way for walkers; it gives no right to ride, and stiles and narrow gates will often prevent you from doing so anyway. However, the landowner can give you permission to ride on them, and some ancient bridleways are still incorrectly recorded as footpaths. This means that in a few cases you can ride a route shown as a public footpath, but you should first check with local riders and the council to be sure.

Public bridleways: You have a legally protected right to ride these routes; bridleways are also shared with walkers and pedal cyclists.

Restricted by-ways: You have a legally protected right to use these too, as do walkers, pedal cyclists and horse-drawn vehicles.

By-ways open to all traffic: You have the right to ride these as they are usually ancient roads that have not been modernized. Car drivers and motorcyclists also have a legal right to use these, although doing so in practice can be difficult.

Roads used as a public path: On out-of-date maps and signs you may see this obsolete phrase. Such routes have now been reclassified; check locally for more information on who can use them now.

Other lanes and tracks: You may have the right to ride these – check locally with other riders and the local council. They include the following:

Yellow roads: You almost always have the right to ride these minor roads coloured in yellow on Explorer maps.

White roads: These are the tracks shown on Explorer maps where the area between the walls or fences has not been coloured in – hence the term 'white road'. Although white roads that just stop at farms and fields usually don't have access rights, those that link public roads and bridleways may well be ancient rights of way that you can use.

Green lanes: People often use this term to describe ancient grass-covered country lanes; this is no proof in itself that you can ride there.

Other routes with public access (ORPAs): These are shown on Explorer maps as green dots. Whilst public access exists on them, the local council can't say precisely who for. Many will be available for horse riders.

● If evidence comes to light that a public right of way is incorrectly recorded – for example, an ancient bridleway is registered as a public footpath – it can be reopened and protected as a bridleway; your local council or bridleways officer can give you more advice.

Definitive Maps

The local council keeps legally binding definitive maps; these are the best guide as to what public rights of way exist, although underfunding means that many still contain errors and omissions.

Common Land

While there is now a right to walk on most common land, there are far fewer opportunities for riders, although some fantastic areas of common land are available. The local council keeps a record of all common land, and can tell you of any areas that are open to riders.

Horse riders in England can readily find where common land exists on the government's website (www.magic.gov.uk), although you will still need to check with the local council as to whether you have a right to ride there.

Village Greens

Village greens are smaller versions of common land and receive very similar legal protection. In some cases they can also provide useful riding opportunities, such as a shortcut away from a busy road junction. As with commons, find out more from the local council. Because many other people use village greens, you must ensure you don't disrupt other activities, or give riders a bad name – for example, by riding across a cricket pitch.

Beaches and the Seashore

There is no general right of access to beaches and the seashore in England and Wales, and even where there is access, local councils can impose restrictions such as banning horse riding on popular beaches and fining those who do not comply.

However, there are many beaches where horses are traditionally ridden; usually the difficulty is getting to them from adjacent land, unless a road or bridleway leads there. The Marine and Coastal Access Act 2009 is creating an access corridor along almost all of England's coastline, and access to the coast in Wales is also being improved. While these improvements are for walkers, they may in time indirectly help riders, if hitherto obstructed routes on to beaches are opened up. It may also give a better opportunity for agreeing permissive access with the landowner.

ACCESS RIGHTS IN SCOTLAND

Thanks to the Land Reform (Scotland) Act 2003, the theoretical opportunities for off-road riding in Scotland are now better than anywhere else in the United Kingdom. But underfunding and lack of gates and connecting routes means that in practical terms it is often more difficult to use your access rights than south of the border. So just as in England, you need to know the many different ways that access is provided in Scotland, and again do some detective work to find out where it is physically possible to ride.

Public Rights of Way

Despite the general right of access to land in Scotland, rights of way are still very important, as they are more permanent, better defined and less liable to temporary closure. Crucially they also often provide the only legally protected route past rural homes, gardens and buildings, and without them access to the wider countryside beyond would be impossible without the landowner's permission.

The distinction between who can use which public rights of way in Scotland, and the system to record them, is poor compared to England and Wales. If a right of way in Scotland has been traditionally used by horse riders for centuries, they have a legally protected right to use it, but this is not always easy to assess. And unlike in England and Wales, a public right of way in Scotland can cease to exist if it has not been used for many years. For these reasons, public rights of way are not specifically identified as such on Ordnance Survey maps in Scotland.

In general, a visible route may well be a public right of way if it links two public places (including, for example, other lanes and roads) and has been openly used for over twenty years. Asking around locally can be a real help, although some riders and landowners may be mistaken about the law or what rights exist. Other sources of information concerning public rights of way include the following:

- Local councils – arranging to look at their maps can be really worthwhile.
- Core paths plans – these will show some, although not all, rights of way in the area; these are sometimes available on line.
- Scotways (Scottish Rights of Way and Access Society, see Further Information) – this charity keeps the National Catalogue of Rights of Way in partnership with government countryside advisers Scottish Natural Heritage. Scotways is also working on a project to promote the heritage of ancient routes, many of which can be ridden.

The Scottish Outdoor Access Code

The Land Reform (Scotland) Act 2003 represents the most extensive provision of access for horse riders anywhere in the United Kingdom, and indeed in much of the world. These access rights are conditional on you riding responsibly, and the Scottish Outdoor Access Code has been developed to help all access users and land managers understand what their responsibilities mean in practice.

The general right of responsible access does not have any boundaries recorded on maps, but is simply described in words, and gives access for horse riders, twenty-four hours a day, over most land and inland water in Scotland including:

- Most paths and tracks.
- Open countryside – hills, mountains, moorland, grassland.
- Land on which crops have not been sown, including stubble.
- Edges of fields where crops are growing or have been sown.
- Grass fields, provided they are not hay or silage fields at a late stage of growth.
- Woodland and forestry.
- Riverbanks, lochs, beaches and the coast.

This right of access includes informal camping for people (but not grazing rights), and hacking out in an organized group. It does not include repetitive schooling or use of other specially provided facilities, such as parking for horse boxes and trailers, or the use of cross-country jumps.

The main places where these access rights do not apply are:

● Houses and gardens.
● Farm steadings, other buildings and associated land.
● Land where crops are growing.
● Land next to a school that is used by the school.
● Sports and playing fields and other recreation land when in use, and if riding on them would interfere with such use.
● Areas where riding would unduly interfere with livestock.
● Golf courses, although you can have a right to cross them as long as you don't interfere with play.
● Places where riding would be dangerous or against the public interest, such as airfields, railways, land used by the military, working quarries and building sites.
● Visitor attractions and other formal facilities where there is an entry charge.
● Routes that riders were charged to use before 2001.

Riders in Scotland have – in theory, at any rate – the best opportunities for off-road riding in the UK.

To ensure you get the most out of your access rights as a horse rider in Scotland and do not cause problems for landowners, wildlife and other access users, it is vital to familiarize yourself with these access rights, as explained in detail on Scottish Natural Heritage's website (*see* Further Information).

The Practical Consequences

These access rights have far-reaching practical consequences, including the following:

- You have a right to ride most tracks that have been constructed on the open hill for game shooting and deerstalking, as long you don't disturb these activities. But unless there is a connecting right of way, you may have difficulty getting to them if you have to pass close to a farm or country house where the general right of access may well not apply for privacy reasons.
- You are responsible for looking behind you to see if your horse is unduly disturbing or damaging the ground; if so, you should cease using that route, especially during wet weather.
- You should not gallop, canter or trot on land if this will cause damage; stay in walk instead.
- Routes that were traditionally footpaths and just for walkers can now be ridden, if you can do so responsibly. However, because many of these routes are still incorrectly signposted as a 'footpath', you may be challenged by landowners or other path users. Contact the local council's access officer if this occurs, and avoid confrontation at the time.
- It is still courteous and responsible to speak with landowners to check if riding in a particular area – especially somewhere new – would cause them problems. Remember that where access rights exist, you are asking about how to ride responsibly, as opposed to asking for permission.
- Some landowners may not recognize the additional access rights given to horse riders by the code, so you may be challenged; politely avoid confrontation and contact the local council's access officer to resolve the issue.
- These access rights are in addition to any other rights and permissions that existed before the Act came into force; landowners are also still free to give permission for activities not covered by the code, such as shooting, motor sports and fishing.

ACCESS IN IRELAND

While many parts of Northern Ireland and the Republic of Ireland have a good network of attractive quiet roads, off-road hacking opportunities are far more limited than on mainland Britain. Public bridleways do exist, but are fewer in number, in part due to insufficient legal backing and funding to record, maintain and assert these rights of way.

Access to beaches is similarly undefined and unprotected, and although tolerated in many places, local council by-laws are increasingly restricting where horse riders can go. British Horse Society (BHS) Ireland has created two toll rides on private estates for use by its members, and efforts have been made by the Countryside Access and Activities Network to increase access through negotiating permissive paths with landowners, but often this only improves access for walkers.

Off-putting notices and the loss of traditional, yet legally unprotected, access have increased in many areas in recent times, so asking around locally is the best thing to do, especially as records of public access are incomplete. BHS Ireland continues to campaign for access for all riders, and particularly deserves your support; its website also includes a great deal of Ireland-specific access information (*see* Further Information).

OTHER PLACES YOU CAN RIDE

Cycle Routes

While as a rule you should keep out of formal cycle lanes in towns, cycle routes in the countryside are a different matter. Just because a route is signposted, promoted and sometimes resurfaced for cyclists (commonly as part of the publicly funded National Cycle Network), it doesn't mean there is no right to ride a horse along it; indeed, many rural cycle routes run on ancient bridleways, so check with the local council about specific routes.

Canals

Horse riders in Scotland are now allowed to ride along canal towpaths, as long as they do so responsibly. Although canal towpaths were originally built to allow horses to pull barges, in England and Wales safety by-laws prohibit riding along them unless a public bridleway is officially recorded; compared to Scotland, this looks increasingly like an arbitrary rule, and could change.

Permissive Access

Public and private landowners are increasingly providing additional access for horse riders. Such permissive access is always in addition to any legal rights of access that already exist – landowners cannot swap rights of access for concessionary routes. A range of conditions can be imposed: it may be free; you may need to get a permit; there may be an annual subscription fee or pay-as-you-go approach; use may be restricted to certain times of the day, week or year; and riders who do not behave responsibly may be banned.

In theory, any landowner can provide additional access for horse riders; such opportunities are most commonly provided by public landowners such as the Forestry Commission, local councils, toll rides, agri-environment schemes, and others, as described below.

The Forestry Commission

The Forestry Commission is one of the biggest public landowners in the United Kingdom. The management of state-owned forests has been devolved to the governments of Scotland, Northern Ireland and Wales, and so differences in approach and funding exist.

In England and Wales there is extensive access for walkers across its land, but more limited access for horse riders, and in some cases a permit system operates. In Scotland, the general right of responsible access includes woodland. Riders still benefit from the Forestry Commission's approach to avoiding unnecessary barriers to access, but may have to pay for extra facilities such as parking.

Use a hi-vis exercise sheet on your horse to increase visibility from the air when riding across land used for low-flying military aircraft exercises. Research shows that you can be spotted up to half a mile earlier, enabling them to take evasive action. (Courtesy RAD Photographic)

In Northern Ireland, the State Forest Service provides designated trails for horse riders in some of its woodlands; a daily fee or annual permit is required.

The Republic of Ireland's public forests are managed by Coilte, the state forestry company (Ireland Forest Service); horse riding is generally prohibited except in a few places.

(*See* Further Information for the relevant websites.)

The Ministry of Defence

While national security means some Ministry of Defence (MoD) land cannot accommodate any public access, there are many places where access for horse riders is allowed, although this may be limited to specific groups or at certain times.

Ordnance Survey maps show some information about MoD land and where managed access is permitted, and you can find out more on their website (see Further Information). MoD land is usually made very clear by off-putting signs, highlighting dangers from unexploded ammunition. Local by-laws define if and when public access can be taken, and horse riders may be restricted to certain tracks. It is well worth checking the actual local by-laws, as sometimes there is more public access than people realize.

MoD land is one of the rare circumstances where public rights of way can be closed due to military operations, although the MoD try to minimize this. Red flags are displayed in the daytime and red lights at night when live firing is taking place, and there is strictly no access to these areas at such times. Even when riding is permitted, you should be alert to any military training in the area, and to military personnel or vehicles that might spook your horse; adjacent areas may also still be used for firearms practice and low-flying jets and helicopters, so consider how your horse may react to sudden loud noises. (*See also* page 77, Countryside Hazards, and page 149, Loose Horse.)

Local Councils

County, district, unitary and parish councils also own significant amounts of land. Some of it will already be managed for recreation, but there can be cases where it is beneficial and reasonable to provide extra access for riders – to avoid a short stretch of busy road, for example.

Individual council officers may not be supportive of requests to increase access on council land, but ultimately the decision rests with council committees, which are comprised of elected councillors. You are quite entitled to contact all your local councillors to discuss opportunities to increase access – you may well find them more inclined to listen around election time!

Where permissive access has been granted, local councils can introduce restrictions and fine people who don't comply. The decision to impose these rests with local councillors, so if you come across a by-law that seems arbitrary or excessive, take it up with your democratically elected representatives.

Other Landowners

Other major landowners in the United Kingdom who provide permissive access for horse riders on their land include the Crown Estate, water companies, the National Trust/National Trust for Scotland, and the Woodland Trust. In the first instance the internet is usually the best place to see where they have land, and their local contact details. Other smaller local landowners may also provide additional access: ask around locally for more information about these.

Toll Rides

These pay-to-ride schemes exist predominantly in England, but are becoming more popular elsewhere. Some riders feel that paying for additional access undermines efforts to make local councils provide a better bridleway network; others take a more pragmatic view, and would rather pay to have additional access now, than wait for a local council to provide it at some time, if ever, in the future.

Pay-to-ride schemes can be across any type of land, and landowners are increasingly looking to national schemes which provide a more consistent approach, and collectively provide better integration between individual landowners. Additional facilities may also be on offer, such as dedicated parking areas, optional cross-country jumps, and accommodation for horse and rider.

Agri-Environment Schemes

Landowners can be paid public money for providing extra access and facilities for riders through these schemes, which aim to encourage them to manage their land in more environmentally friendly ways. The actual scheme names vary, and in most cases access is for walkers only, but some additional access for horse riders is provided. Your local council's access team can help you find out if there are any in your area.

Informal Permitted Access

Sometimes local landowners are happy to allow permissive access for riders in places where access rights don't exist. They may wish to do this in a low-key way, such as agreeing access only for local people. It's their choice, and another good reason for being courteous to land managers. When landowners do provide additional access, it's helpful and fair to suggest they check their public liability insurance cover, because if they are voluntarily providing additional access they may find themselves underinsured. It's also reasonable for them to require riders to have their own third party insurance. There are simple steps a landowner can take to provide permissive access without running the risk of a public right of way being created through prolonged and unopposed use; the local council can advise on this.

TRESPASS

If you ride on land in the UK where you have no right or permission to be, you are technically a trespasser. Trespass is a civil wrong against the landowner, who is entitled to ask you to return to a point where you do have a right or permission to be (for example, a public road or right of way); they can also use reasonable force to make you do so if you refuse. You could also be sued for compensation if your riding has caused damage or financial loss – for example to crops, fences or walls, or to specially managed surfaces such as golf courses.

Contrary to popular belief, you cannot be prosecuted or criminalized for trespass in itself, except where a specific law has been imposed. The latter usually applies to land used for airports, railways and national security (typically land owned by the Ministry of Defence). There

Trespass is generally a civil wrong, although in certain places it is a criminal offence.

will usually be plenty of signs advising you of this on the perimeter of such land.

Sometimes access rights are not accurately recorded and a landowner may regard you as a trespasser, even though you may be entitled to be there. If confronted with this situation, avoid getting into a heated argument, but politely explain that you will contact the local authority access officers to resolve the situation, and leave.

Most landowners are reasonable and respect the law, but a small minority have been known to seek retaliation, so do not offer your contact details, or where your horse is kept. Even if you are a trespasser, as long as you leave when requested, the landowner is not entitled to threaten, injure or abuse you – and if this does occur, report the matter to the police, particularly if a shotgun or other firearm is involved.

FINDING YOUR WAY

Wherever you live, it can take a lot of concerted detective work to find out all the places you can ride, by right or by permission. But the more you start exploring and talking to people, the more access opportunities you'll find.

A good way of recording and sharing information with other riders about riding routes is by using free on-line mapping systems, such as the downloadable programme Google Earth and on-line Google maps (*see* Further Information). These let you superimpose your route information on to maps and aerial photographs; you can add notes about surfaces, gates and other information as well as your own photographs. It's also easy to print off a route map for a given day. The British Horse Society's Emagin mapping database is still in its early stages, but in time will also form a useful resource (*see* Further Information).

Maps

Which Map?

In England, Scotland and Wales the most useful maps to use are the Ordnance Survey 1:25,000 (2.5in to one mile) Explorer maps, which show field boundaries, such as walls or fences, as well as extensive information provided by the local council on public rights of way, and some permissive paths. The OS Landranger maps at 1:50,000 (1.25in to a mile) also show rights of way but are not detailed enough for on-the-ground navigation, although they do give a good initial overview of what access is available. Another option are Harvey 1:25,000 maps, which have a good coverage in many areas; some are specifically produced for horse riders. Harvey and Ordnance Survey maps are available in local bookstores and from on-line retailers such as Amazon.

Riders in other countries also have access to some good quality mapping; most countries have a state mapping agency, which may be a private company or a part of national government. Again, mapping at 1:25,000 is best, although in some areas you may need to make do with 1:50,000 or 1:100,000. A good resource for finding and buying the best available maps from all over the world is Stanford's bookshop in London (*see* Further Information).

Maps to Take Riding

As well as the government's on-line mapping system (www.magic.gov.uk), many other websites provide free, printable extracts of good quality mapping, including Ordnance Survey Explorer maps. As long as these maps are for your own use you are very unlikely to breach any copyright rules. Ordnance Survey and other maps over fifty years old are usually out of copyright, so you can make copies and share them with friends. In many rural areas little will have changed since those older maps were made, although you should check against a modern map and draw on any changes.

Printed extracts or photocopies will be less bulky to carry, easy to refer to, and mean you can avoid damage to expensive purchased maps from rain and constant refolding, leaving them at home for reference use instead. Pop them inside a clear plastic map holder; if it's a route you're likely to ride a lot, laminate them to increase their durability.

Map Reading

Being able to read a map is an exceptionally useful skill. Many local colleges and outdoor education centres run courses, or you may have competent friends who are prepared to teach you. Free map-reading booklets are also available on the Ordnance Survey website (*see* Further Information).

Once you've learnt the basics, go for a walk or cycle. Go somewhere you know first, and compare what you see with what the map shows; then go somewhere new and try navigating using the map to find your way around.

A life-saving map skill is being able to give an accurate grid reference. This is a way of pinpointing where you are, using a unique series of numbers that you can derive from your map. Quoting this location code will help emergency services find you in remote areas, and assist local councils in locating any problems you report. For more information, refer to the Ordnance Survey's free booklet on using the national grid, available on its website.

Compass and Global Positioning System (GPS)

When venturing into wilder and more isolated areas, you will also need a compass. It will of course be pointless if you don't know how to use it, so when you buy one, ask shop staff for advice on this, as well as the best type for your purposes. Instructional books are also available, and plenty of information and tutorials can be found on the internet. Spend some time using it with a map, ensuring you are quite competent before needing to use it for real.

If you like gadgets, you can invest in a hand-held or wrist-mounted global positioning system, or GPS. These receive signals from satellites orbiting the earth, providing you with navigational features which allow you to find a location, or return to your starting point following your original route. It is also possible to buy mobile phones that have GPS systems and satellite navigation – but as technology can sometimes fail or become damaged, it is essential to carry a compass with you as well, as a back-up.

Promoted Routes and Trails

If you don't want to do a great deal of preparatory research, a good way to explore new areas is to ride one of the promoted routes for horse riders. These range from government-supported recreational routes (called National Trails in England and Wales – although not all are for horses) to trails developed by local councils and riders' groups. They are often listed on websites (*see* Further Information).

Promoted routes often have their own guidebooks and leaflets listing details such as where you can park, and giving essential emergency information. Given their higher level of usage, local councils will also often improve the safety of these routes. They are usually well signposted, and may have special waymark arrows to ensure you don't get lost; nevertheless, carry a local map in case the route is blocked or you need to detour because of bad weather or in the event of an emergency.

It's also worth looking at off-road cycling guides, as in most cases horse riders can also use these routes. Remember that the routes are selected for two wheels rather than four feet, so be prepared to walk sections which may be too steep for horses, or which are likely to be damaged by hooves. And as you are highly likely to meet cyclists, make sure you and your horse are prepared for them.

NOTES FOR RIDE ESCORTS

- You should know all the routes thoroughly before taking sole charge of a ride, including the names of fields and local landmarks so that in the event of an emergency you can give precise directions to your location.
- Familiarity with the various routes will also enable you to judge time and pace reasonably accurately so rides can be kept running on time.
- Even if you know an area well, it's always useful to have a map extract with you in case you need to take a shortcut or give a grid reference to the emergency services.

OBSTRUCTIONS

Public Rights of Way

Although a map may show a route in great detail, it won't tell you what state it is in or if it's blocked, so always have a back-up plan just in case you find your way impassable.

In general it is an offence for anyone to make a highway, whether a tarmac road or grassy bridleway, more difficult or dangerous to use than it traditionally was. It is the job of local councils to enforce this rule, although council chiefs frequently do not have either the staff or the funding to deal with all the problems that currently exist.

This general rule – that public rights of way should remain open and available for the public to use at any time – is not always clear-cut once you start looking at individual routes and situations. For example, a public bridleway running across fields can be ploughed, although it must be put back in good order within a few days and the path surface then kept clear as the crop grows. Rights of way around the edges of fields, on the other hand, should not be ploughed, and in most cases doing so can be a criminal offence.

Local councils can also authorize the temporary closure or diversion of rights of way for legitimate reasons (such as laying cables, drainage and building works), although the paths must be restored to as good a condition as they were previously. Councils can also permanently close public rights of way, although local bridleways groups will usually be consulted about such orders; also the procedures to do so are complex and not guaranteed to succeed.

Generally, councils have a legal duty to maintain public bridleways and rights of way just as much as main roads, but as this duty is not dependent on whether they can afford to do so, most will have a priority scheme whereby roads will take precedence. This does not, however, entitle them to neglect their duty to

In the UK there can be a big difference between having the right to ride a route, and being physically able to do so.

maintain public rights of way indefinitely, and they could in theory be taken to court for failure to do so.

Councils do have a general power of improvement, and can at their discretion make routes easier to use than they traditionally were, but whether they take action very much depends on local circumstances. For a more detailed practical overview of rights of way law in England and Wales, download or order a free copy of CA210 *Managing Public Access from Natural England*. A guide to the law in Scotland is available from Scotways (*see* Further Information).

- County councils and unitary authorities are in most cases ultimately responsible for public rights of way, but they may have an agreement with a national park, parish or district council to maintain paths; such arrangements can vary over time. Any local council contact point or helpline should, however, be able to tell you which council or department you should contact at a local level if you encounter a problem. Your local bridleways groups may also have a list of who to contact.

Who is Responsible?

The local council is responsible for putting right problems caused by natural forces such as rain or snow, and wear and tear caused by path users.

The owners of the land underneath and on either side of a public right of way are responsible for ensuring their activities do not make the path more difficult (for example, by damaging the surface with a tractor) or more dangerous to use (for example by putting up barbed wire or spraying with chemicals). The council has a legal duty to ensure they comply.

If you are injured or suffer a financial loss (such as ripping your coat on barbed wire) due to an unlawful problem on a public right of way, you may be able to sue the person responsible – usually the council or the landowner – for damages. In some cases they could be prosecuted for breaking the law.

Misleading and Intimidating Notices

It is an offence for a landowner to put up or maintain notices that intimidate or deter the public from going where they have a right to be; these should be reported. While in some cases the issue is very clear cut – for instance a sign saying 'No public right of way – keep out', in other cases it is not so clear. For example, signs that are off-putting to many people, such as 'Private road', 'Bull in field' or 'Unsuitable for horse riders', may be acceptable in legal terms because they are statements of fact and do not directly say you have no right to be there. The best way to avoid any confusion is for the local council to clearly signpost public rights of way and other routes.

Problems on Other Routes

While the rules about what is and isn't allowed on public rights of way are complicated, on other types of access matters can be even less straightforward. Whatever the route type, it should not become more dangerous to use, although do remember that one solution to problems on permissive routes is to simply close them. Even if the problem is not the responsibility of the local council, contacting them is usually the best place to start as they will often know who to contact.

Loss of Access Rights

In Scotland, under certain circumstances a

public right of way may be lost if it has fallen into disuse for a period of time. This principle does not currently apply in England and Wales, although proposals to change the law to allow this are being considered. Currently, if the route was a public bridleway in England and Wales at some time in the past – even 200 years ago – it continues to be a public bridleway today, unless a formal legal process has been completed to extinguish it. There is also an oft-repeated myth that rights of way need to be used at least once a year to keep them open. Again, while there is no formal legal justification for this, it is absolutely true that the best way to keep routes open for riders is to make sure they are regularly used.

Right to Remove Obstructions and Deviate

If you come across an obstruction on a public right of way, the law allows two 'self-help' options: the right to deviate around the obstruction, and the right to remove enough of the obstruction to continue on your way. So if the branch of a tree had fallen across the public bridleway you are riding along, and you had a saw with you, you'd be entitled to cut away just enough of it to get past. Alternatively, if the route was unfenced, or gates allowed you to go briefly in and out of an adjacent field to get around the obstruction, that would usually also be acceptable.

These options do need to be exercised with great caution, especially when riding a new route for the first time. Cutting a hole in a fence you believed was blocking a public bridleway could allow livestock to escape on to a road and cause an accident; and if you had misread your map and the fence was not actually blocking a public right of way you could be prosecuted for criminal damage.

Therefore, unless you really have absolutely no alternative, in many cases it is often best to

retrace your steps and go another way, and report the matter to the local council. If the obstruction means your ride becomes more hazardous – having to detour on to a busy narrow road, for example – do make that clear, as councils will often deal more quickly with obstructions if a safety issue is involved.

Reporting Problems

You can make it easier for the local council to take action by providing accurate details about what the problem is, and where it is located. Giving an accurate grid reference is really useful, as is taking digital photographs of the problem.

Be polite and not too pushy when first reporting a problem, but always ask for an anticipated timescale for action. Some councils have hundreds of outstanding problems to deal with, and may have a formal prioritization policy – if so, ask for a copy. If told it will take many months – or even years – to address, don't take your frustration out on the council staff. They can only be as effective as the resources available allow, and they are probably as frustrated as you! Ask for details of the council's complaints procedure, and contact your local BHS access officer, who may be able to give you more advice.

Barbed Wire

Barbed wire can present particular problems for riders, and there is often far more of it alongside rights of way than the law allows. It is a criminal offence for a landowner to put up or maintain barbed wire so that it makes a public right of way more dangerous or damaging to use. Whether the wire breaks the law in practice will depend on the particular circumstances of the path: thus if it were quite narrow, or the barbed wire were wrapped around a gate, it's far more likely to be unlawful. Report such problems to the local council, who can then take up the matter with the landowner.

IMPROVING LOCAL RIDING OPPORTUNITIES

Do consider supporting your local bridleways group: as well as helping to protect access which currently exists, such groups also campaign for better access and off-road alternatives in dangerous areas. They are also concerned with safety issues that impact on the usage of rights of way by horse riders, such as nearby clay pigeon shooting, or the need for rider-friendly Pegasus crossings on busy roads.

These groups are usually the first point of contact for local councils seeking riders' views on any access changes and improvements. It is also a legal obligation for local councils in England, Scotland and Wales to run local access forums, at which riders' representatives play an important part in helping improve access for all riders.

Volunteers are always needed both at local and regional level, and getting involved needn't be hugely time-consuming and demanding. Some groups are affiliated to the BHS and others are independently run: if there isn't currently a group in your area, you might like to team up with other riders to form one. Working together as a group will carry far more weight than a lone voice when pressing for changes or improvements – and many hands make light work!

COURTESY

Always be polite and considerate to others you meet; it takes little effort and helps promote tolerance and goodwill towards horse riders. If people show discourtesy to you, it may be through ignorance about horses rather than being intentional. Deliberate or not, being

Rider-friendly Pegasus crossings show a green horse and rider when it is safe to cross, and a red one when you should stay put.

abusive is likely to inflame matters further and certainly won't encourage them to be more considerate in the future. It is advisable to observe the following code of conduct:

- Always acknowledge motorists who stop or slow down for you by raising a hand. If you need to keep both hands on the reins, show your appreciation with a smile and nod of your head instead.
- If you meet another rider, warn her of your approach and intention to overtake. If asked to wait for a safer stretch of road, do so. When ready, pass at a steady speed and at a safe distance.

● Show good manners to landowners and their staff. You may need their help in an emergency or to increase riding opportunities in the future.
● Verbally thank walkers who step off the track for you, put their dogs on leads or show any other courtesy towards you. Always pass in walk, giving adequate space: remember that some people may be afraid of horses.
● Don't splatter walkers with mud or water by trotting past them.
● Be brave enough to speak to other riders who may not realize they are being inconsiderate; they may simply be copying the bad example set by less well mannered riders.

Route Sharing

It is exceptionally rare for a route to be exclusively for equestrians. In almost every case, walkers and cyclists are also entitled to use the same routes, and it is essential to show them the same courtesy as you would want for yourself. Even if someone is technically trespassing on a riders-only route, you must still pass with courtesy and care – though you may politely want to direct them to where they have a right to be.

While in theory there are different rules as to who should give way to whom on different routes, always pass others in walk, and be prepared to stop. Even if somebody else should give way to you, don't put yourself or your horse at risk by assuming they will do so.

'Leave No Trace'

The seven principles of 'leave no trace' are an internationally accepted way to help anyone exploring the outdoors to remain a welcome visitor and to protect the environment for generations to come. As a rider this means the following:

1. Plan ahead and prepare
● Find out in advance where you can ride.
● Take responsibility for your own safety.
● Check the weather and any seasonal restrictions.
● Prepare for emergencies and hazards.
● Take all essential clothing and safety equipment.
● Avoid routinely riding in large groups and at busy times if you can.

2. Ride on suitable surfaces
● Avoid riding when and where you will damage the surface.
● Adjust where you ride to reflect the seasons and ground conditions.
● Stick to designated routes unless you are permitted to ride on open ground.
● Report maintenance problems to trail managers (usually the local council in the UK).
● Avoid repetitive schooling on the same ground unless you have permission.

3. Dispose of waste properly
● Take all your litter home or place it in a bin if provided.
● Ideally take a sealable bag for toilet paper or other hygiene products.
● Look round for litter before leaving any rest stops, and pick it up.
● Kick horse poo to the side on narrow and multi-use routes where it might be a problem for others.

4. Leave as you find
● Don't interfere with or damage walls, fences, buildings, farming or forestry equipment.
● Leave gates as you find them.
● Don't build jumps or other features without permission.
● Leave all features of the environment as they are, including flowers, animals, rocks and plants.

5. Minimize the effects of fire
- Make doubly sure any smoking materials are thoroughly extinguished.
- Don't smoke at all in areas of high fire risk.
- Only make campfires or use barbecues where you have permission.
- Promptly report any uncontrolled fires you see.

6. Respect farm animals and wildlife
- Pass livestock and wildlife at a walk.
- Never feed wildlife or domesticated animals unless you have permission.
- Heed requests to avoid sensitive places and times for wildlife.
- Report incidents or suspicious activity that could be damaging to wildlife or farm animals.

7. Be considerate of others
- Respect the enjoyment and livelihoods of other visitors, residents, farmers and other businesses.
- Minimize any interference with other people's activities.
- Be courteous and friendly; give way to others and pass at walk.
- Park with consideration; don't block gateways, narrow lanes or access points.
- Avoid making excessive noise.

Individual countries incorporate these principles into a nationally relevant set of rules, often called the 'Countryside Code'. The codes for England, Scotland, Wales and Ireland do vary; you can find the version for your area in the Further Information section on page 170 of this book.

NOTES FOR RIDE ESCORTS

Remain calm at all times and set a good example to others. No matter how tempting, do not shout, swear or gesture insultingly at anyone: try to remain civil because your actions reflect not just on yourself, but may affect the reputation of your employer and riding centre, and can offend clients, too.

4 Terrain

RIDING UP HILLS

Long inclines can be useful for increasing fitness and stamina, but are more tiring for your horse than working on a level surface – something to bear in mind if you are planning to take him for a day ride or a holiday in a hilly area. The longer and steeper a gradient is, the harder it will be. Some horses may try and rush at the beginning of the slope, but gradually run out of steam: try to maintain an even rhythm and speed, and be ready to use your legs if he begins to flag.

When tackling very steep hills either walk up, or if your horse is fit and the surface suitable, canter up, as trotting will place an increased strain on the sacroiliac, hip and hock joints. Canter is often the best gait when riding up sand-dunes, as the momentum helps to keep you moving; going at walk may mean you just slide back down. Your horse may also decide this is the best speed, but don't go faster or further than you can see to stop in safety; there could be a horse coming the other way or a child making a sandcastle just beyond the top of the dune.

Position when riding up a hill.

Position when riding down a slope.

Incline your upper body forward with your weight positioned over your horse's centre of gravity so you are in balance with him; this will make it easier for him to engage his back and hindquarters to power himself up the hill. Don't over-exaggerate it, as this will unbalance him and cause him to struggle. The more supple you are in your hip, knee and ankle joints, the easier you will find this; if you are very stiff in these areas, ask your riding teacher to show you some suppling exercises to practise in between rides. Maintain the rein contact, but allow enough length of rein that your horse can stretch and use his head and neck. Don't pull on the reins or use them for support – take a handful of mane or hold the neckstrap to help you stay in balance.

Unless there is a properly defined track or path to follow, ride straight up steep slopes rather than tackling them at an angle, as this will make it easier for your horse to keep his footing and his quarters engaged. Where slopes are very steep or have a loose surface, it may be safer to dismount and lead your horse.

RIDING DOWN HILLS

Some horses are more surefooted and confident about tackling downhill gradients than others. If your horse tends to crab sideways when going down slopes it may be due to discomfort from saddle fit or back problems.

Steep descents should only be attempted when both horse and rider can cope with shallow ones. They increase the strain placed on the horse's front legs; more novice riders and very young or old horses may also find it hard to keep their balance. On very steep slopes, especially if the surface is loose, it may be safer to dismount and lead (*see* page 63, Loose Surfaces).

Unless there is a properly defined path or track to follow, always move in a straight line down hills; moving at an angle increases the risk of your horse falling. Concentration and balance are needed, and as he makes his descent, your horse will tuck his quarters beneath him to help support his weight. Be patient if he finds it difficult and needs to take smaller steps. Stay in walk, but be prepared – although he may take the first part steadily enough, as he gets closer to the bottom he may begin to rush, so ensure you have sufficient rein contact to maintain control.

Keeping your upper body perpendicular and looking ahead, not downwards, should put you in a good balance with your horse. You will need to lengthen your reins, but keep enough contact that although he can use his head and neck to assist with his balance, you can guide and when necessary use half-halts to rebalance him. Keep all your joints flexed and flexible so they can act efficiently as shock absorbers and help you maintain a stable position; heels can be a little deeper than usual to help with security, although don't force them down as this will lock the joints. Support your weight on your thighs and lightly on your seat too, not just on the stirrups, as this increases your security and makes it easier for you to use your legs.

Hovering Trot Exercise

Practising this exercise in a safe enclosed area at home teaches you how to let hip, knee and ankle joints work as shock absorbers, and develops lower leg stability, so is useful for improving balance and security. As well as helping you deal with gradients, it's also good preparation for learning to jump, or for adopting a forward seat for cantering and galloping.

● Shorten your stirrups between one and three holes from your normal flatwork length.

Hovering trot.

● Ask for an active but regular trot. Once established, and using a handful of mane or the neckstrap to help you balance, adopt a position with your seat still close to, but slightly raised out of the saddle so you are neither sitting nor rising. To keep your balance you will need to incline your upper body forwards slightly, and keep hip, knee and ankle joints flexed but not fixed so they can absorb the 'bounce' of the trot. Let the heel drop slightly lower than usual; you may find it helps if you push your seat back a little so it acts as a counterbalance to your upper body.

● If you lean too far forwards, or let your lower leg slip forwards or backwards, or stiffen through any joints, you'll find you will lose your balance and flop back into the saddle. You'll know when you get it right as it will feel effortless and easy to maintain.

NOTES FOR RIDE ESCORTS

- If you have the opportunity, teaching the 'hovering trot' exercise can be a helpful pre-ride preparation before tackling hills.
- Don't let groups get too strung out, as it increases the likelihood of horses rushing as they get near the bottom of a hill. Warn riders that this may be a possibility, so they are not taken by surprise.

LOOSE SURFACES

Keep your horse in walk when riding over loose surfaces such as shale or scree, as it is the most stable as well as the slowest gait. Loose surfaces are especially treacherous when on sloping ground, whether going up or down, and it may be safer to dismount and lead your horse. If it's necessary to cross a loose-surfaced gradient at an angle, stay to the uphill side of him when leading so he doesn't slip on to you. If you decide to remain in the saddle, be ready to do an emergency dismount if your horse does begin to fall (*see* page 143, Horse Falls).

SLIPPERY SURFACES

Ice can be a major hazard during freezing weather: the fact that it isn't always visible only adds to the danger, and the first you may know of the presence of 'black ice' is when your horse slips on it. Try to avoid going out on roads when they are likely to be icy as the possibility of your horse slipping isn't the only danger – there is also the risk of traffic skidding, losing control and colliding with you. If you do have to go out, wait until as late as possible in the

Wet weather can make some surfaces more slippery. Take care also when emerging from tracks on to roads: as well as passing traffic, the sudden change in footing may be hazardous. (Courtesy RAD Photographic)

day so the sun has a chance to thaw any ice – but beware shaded areas of road which may still be frozen.

Keeping close to roadside edges may help if grit has accumulated there, but bear in mind that the road camber can mean icy puddles there, too. Use grass verges where possible and where it is safe to do so (*see* page 68, Grass Verges), put knee boots on your horse (*see* page 35, Leg Protection), and ask your farrier's advice about using frost nails or road studs (see below Improving Grip). Stay in walk and if your horse starts to lose his footing, sit very quietly so you don't interfere with his balance, and slip your feet from the stirrups ready to jump clear if necessary.

Ice is not the only slippery surface you may encounter. Mossy ground and short grass can be just as treacherous when wet, and when dry as well if the ground beneath is hard. Some metalled roads can be as much of a problem, too; and watch out for shiny patches, spilt diesel, inspection covers, drainage grilles, and road markings, especially when they are wet. The central part of a lane, between the tracks of car tyres, may also provide more grip – but only ride there if you can do so safely. Dismount and lead your horse if necessary until you reach a safer stretch of road.

● The state of your horse's shoes can have a bearing on how slippery a road appears to be: if they are very worn your horse will be more likely to slip.

Improving Grip

You can increase the amount of grip your horse's feet get by using non-slip nails, road studs or plugs, or shoes with tungsten carbide crystals welded to them. However, improving grip can have drawbacks as it can cause jarring of the legs – a small amount of sliding as the feet touch the ground is thought to play an important part in helping to reduce concussion. Ask your farrier about the pros and cons, and what is best for your horse.

SOFT AND BOGGY GROUND

Soft going can vary from wet, cloggy ploughland to soft, dry sand or shingle dunes, all of which can be very tiring for your horse, so be considerate and keep to a steady walk.

Off-road tracks that get a lot of use from horse riders can rapidly deteriorate in wet weather, becoming poached and sometimes getting very deep and boggy. Take an alternative route if possible so you don't cause further damage or risk an overreach or a strain, or a shoe getting sucked off.

If riding in an area known to have bogs, mires or quicksand, seek out local advice as to where it is and isn't safe to ride if you are unfamiliar with the area yourself. These locations can change from year to year, so even if you have ridden there previously, still check and get up-to-date guidance.

Bogs are a common hazard in moorland areas: keep to marked tracks wherever possible, and skirt carefully round any boggy ground – look out for areas of dark brown wet peat, bright green areas of sphagnum moss, or areas of vegetation such as deergrass, hare's tail cottongrass, reeds, sedges and other bog-loving plants that indicate soft ground. Your horse may find himself trapped in treacherous going elsewhere, too – beaches, riverbeds, marshland, and places where underground springs bubble up towards the surface can become saturated by water and turn into a sucking morass. These vary in size and can look like solid ground, so always move with caution in such places; keep on marked tracks where they exist, and heed local advice. If your horse is suddenly reluctant to move forwards, it may be that he is responding to a change in footing which you can't feel, rather than being disobedient.

Dismount and lead him so you can check the ground ahead on foot yourself.

If he does step into a bog or area of quicksand, ask him to back up immediately; if he's floundered forwards into it with all four legs, dismount so as to remove your weight from his back. Encourage him to extricate himself, taking care as he may lurch and flounder unpredictably; but if he has gone in deep and is unable to get clear by his own efforts, contact the emergency services immediately. Time may be of the essence, as he could be in danger from an incoming tide or at risk of hypothermia. While waiting for help to arrive, try to keep him calm and still, as struggling will make him sink deeper and will quickly exhaust him.

Maintenance of Surfaces

In the United Kingdom, local councils usually have a duty to maintain the surfaces of public rights of way 'in character'. If a right of way that has traditionally been dry all year round starts to become boggy because it's being ridden, they usually have a duty to repair the surface and stop it deteriorating. Report it to the council,

and if action isn't taken you can make a formal complaint and in some cases even take them to court. However, if a route has always been boggy at certain times – for example across land that floods near a river – councils are usually not obliged to make it usable all year round, although they can do so if they wish. Responsibility for maintaining the surfaces of other routes varies; check with the local council.

HARD GROUND

Most riders are taught early on in their riding career that it's not good to do too much trotwork on road surfaces, and that you should never, ever canter on them. This isn't just because they can be slippery but because their hard and unyielding surface causes shock waves to travel up the limbs.

Horses with thin soles and low heels will be more susceptible to the effects of concussion, as will those with more upright foot and limb conformation, which is less good at shock absorption. Friction can increase the effects of concussion, so if considering using road nails or anything that gives shoes a better grip, discuss the matter, and whether it's suitable for your horse, with your farrier.

Roads aren't the only hard surface you'll encounter: in summer the ground can become baked to a concrete-like hardness, while during the winter, freezing conditions can lead to equally unforgiving going. When unlevel ground is dried or frozen it can add to the problems, causing tripping and bruised soles. Periods of wet weather can also wash away surfaces, leaving stony and flinty areas uncovered.

The first indication that your horse may be feeling the effects of hard ground is a shorter, stilted, more pottery stride, but excessive concussion can have serious long-term consequences and can lead to laminitis and to permanent damage to joints and bones.

NOTES FOR RIDE ESCORTS

Report back to the centre manager any areas where the ridden track is being damaged by repeated use; at best it can cause bad publicity for the centre, and at worst it could lead to an injury. The centre manager should consider using alternative routes at certain times of the year and discuss it with the landowner and local council. Offering to be flexible with regard to routes can do a lot to ensure guests always get a good experience and a warm welcome from landowners.

Prevention as far as possible is the best policy: ensure good hoof balance through regular attention from the farrier, and use grass verges where possible. When you have to ride on hard ground, walk when you can, and when you do trot, keep your horse balanced and steady, as letting him become fast and unbalanced increases the amount of concussion.

UNKNOWN GOING

Don't be tempted to rush when crossing unknown areas as there may be hazards such as rabbit holes, land drains, depressions in the ground, or tussocky and boggy areas which aren't visible until you are on top of them. Unexpected changes between soft and firm going can also take your horse by surprise, causing him to miss his footing or twist and strain joints.

Pay attention to where your horse is going so you can pick the best route for him; just because something is right in front of him doesn't mean he can see it properly, as the length of his nose creates a 'blind spot' just in front of it.

Where ground is unlevel – whether undulating, rutted, tussocky or covered with tree roots – the more balanced your horse is, and the better developed his awareness of where his feet are, the better he will cope. Working over poles at home can help with this, laying them out at random and at angles to each other rather than in ordered rows. Start with just a few poles, gradually increasing the number and complexity as he grows more confident and able, and raising the ends of some as well. (*See also* page 162, Stumbling.)

Polework exercises can help improve your horse's surefootedness. (Bob Atkins, courtesy Horse & Rider *magazine)*

WOODLAND

Woodland rides can be wonderfully cool places to ride during the summer, but keep your wits about you, as piles of leaves can conceal depressions in the ground, and tree roots that may trip the unwary. Keep an eye out for fallen branches, and duck forwards to pass safely beneath low-growing ones; be aware that your shift of weight forwards may be interpreted by some horses as a cue to go faster. If you are with other riders, don't get too close to the horse in front as you won't be able to see the ground ahead clearly – neither do you want a whippy branch suddenly springing back in your face.

Where roads pass through wooded areas, the dappled shade cast by the leafy canopy overhead can make it less easy for motorists to see you, so hi-vis clothing is a 'must'. Your horse's eyes take longer than yours to adjust to changes in light conditions, so he may be slower than you to notice hazards ahead. It may also make him a little more spooky – be patient, reassure him, and go slowly to give his vision more time to adjust. Fallen leaves can also make roads very slippery in autumn and winter.

Woodlands are best avoided during high winds when there may be a danger of falling branches; and stear clear of any areas where tree felling and coppicing is going on.

Watch out for fallen branches, tree roots and other hazards on the ground.

NOTES FOR RIDE ESCORTS

Twisty woodland tracks may obscure your vision of the riders following behind you. Stop wherever there is a natural clearing or glade to check that everyone is still present and correct: when a rear escort is present, equipping them with a walkie talkie (*see* page 109, Riding in Company) or a whistle to blow means you can be alerted if anyone gets into difficulties.

● Badgers can excavate huge underground chambers and passages, sometimes directly under paths and tracks. Look out for the mound of excavated earth and go past carefully at a walk.

OPEN SPACES

An open expanse of green turf can look inviting to canter on, but frequently that close-cropped grass is due to rabbits – meaning that rabbit holes are likely to be present, which could result in a nasty fall should your horse put a foot down one. By all means enjoy a canter, but check the ground ahead first by walking your intended route. Looking out for the entrances to rabbit burrows can also help you predict areas where solid-looking ground under your horse could collapse into the tunnels beneath.

As well as rabbits, sheep may be grazing; if the ground is undulating and they are in a dip you may not notice them until you are quite close. They will usually scatter out of your way as you approach, but ride through slowly and calmly at a walk so you don't distress them. Sheep may also spook your horse if they suddenly emerge from behind bushes without warning.

Moorland

As well as open downland, the UK has large tracts of moorland which can offer spectacular views as well as challenging terrain to ride over. Some tracks can be stony, and you may have to negotiate features such as rivers, fords, bridges and gates (*see* page 85, Bridges and Underpasses, and page 83, Gates). There may also be areas of bog, which can be easy to stray into (*see* page 64, Soft and Boggy Ground) and other hazards you may be less prepared for, such as ground-nesting birds launching themselves into the air from just under your horse's feet. At certain times of year there may be shooting, and in some areas low-flying jets and helicopters taking part in military exercises (*see* page 77, Countryside Hazards).

Although some routes will be well travelled and well marked, others may be faint and hard to see, so good map-reading and compass skills are important, as well as knowing the

procedure in the event of becoming lost (*see* page 148, Lost).

Because there are few natural features that act as a windbreak, open moorland can be cold for riding, so wrap up well. Lack of features can also make map reading more difficult, as can poor visibility – fog and mist can often descend very quickly in such areas – and if caught in a thunderstorm you may be more exposed to the danger of lightning strike. Listen to, and take heed of weather forecasts, and if necessary either take a different route or have a day off.

GRASS VERGES

Grass verges alongside roads are traditionally and legally as much a part of a public highway as the tarmac surface the cars drive on, and often provide a valuable – and at times life-saving – alternative for more vulnerable road users. Obstructing a verge is as much a criminal offence as blocking the road: sometimes they are unlawfully neglected by local councils, either due to lack of maintenance or because home owners have been allowed to turn them into gardens or car parking areas, or to obstruct them with fences and large rocks. This can lead you to assume that you can't use them, whereas the truth is that although councils can permit some limited cultivation of verges by householders, a formal licence needs to be issued.

In some cases, local councils will make by-laws banning riding on certain verges, in which case signs should be erected to this effect. If your council tries to introduce such a ban, make sure you contact your local councillors and ask them what they are going to do to make the roads safer for displaced riders. Sometimes 'no horse riding' notices are erected by councils or home owners, which have no legal basis: check with the local council, and if the signs are misleading ask that they be removed.

Safety

Irrespective of your rights to ride on verges, always do so with consideration for others, and do not churn up the surface. Also proceed cautiously, because if overgrown, verges can conceal all sorts of hazards such as drainage ditches, broken glass and other rubbish. Even where they are mown there may be pipes, cables and metal connection boxes on or just below the surface, so never go faster than a walk.

Furthermore verges can give a false sense of security, and encourage motorists to drive past you faster than they would if you were on the main carriageway. If alongside a hedge, a bird flying out or any noise or movement from it could cause your horse to spook and jump into the road and into the path of oncoming traffic. Also lamp-posts and signs positioned on the grass verge may require you to step on to the road in order to get past them, which may be a manouvre fraught with hazard if there is much traffic. If a verge is narrow there will be little margin for error if your horse spooks, in which case it may be safer to stay on the road.

Pavements

The surfaced pavement (also called a footway) provided for walkers alongside a road is not the same as the verge: it is against the law to ride along it, although crossing it to get to the grassy verge is perfectly reasonable. The police could in theory take action if you did ride along a pavement, although if doing so was safer than riding along the road in some places, you might want to take the risk. Never ride on the pavement if it will endanger pedestrians, and if your horse fouls the footway, kick the droppings on to the verge or the edge of the road if you can do so safely at the time – otherwise return later with a shovel.

SAFETY

The safety of any water crossing can vary by the hour due to changes in water flow, scouring of the riverbed, and debris such as tree branches and discarded shopping trolleys. The rate at which the water flows is more of a risk factor than the depth alone; although deep, still water can be a challenge for some horses, it can be far less dangerous than fast-flowing water that only comes halfway up his legs. A fast flow can sweep him off his feet, or make it impossible for him to recover if he stumbles. It is also more likely to wash you downstream if you fall.

Many fords have a graduated gauge at the side showing how deep the water is: remember that recent rain can make a big difference in a short space of time, and that fords near the coast may be affected by tides. If in doubt, take another route.

● To check if a verge is a part of the highway which you are entitled to ride along, contact the Highway Records Officer from the local council.

WATER

Going for a splash through some water can be a fun way of cooling down in warm weather – but if it's something outside your horse's experience so far, he may be reluctant to get his feet wet at first. Many horses are suspicious and very cautious about entering water, so be patient if this is the case as it is usually quite genuine fear.

Preparation Pays

Before you can introduce your horse to water you first need to find a suitable place. You may know of a ford or shallow stream nearby, but if not, try hiring a cross-country course with a water complex.

The approach into the water should be firm underfoot and have a shallow gradient; if it's slippery or a steep drop it will add to your horse's reluctance. The base also needs to be level, firm and predictable, and not boggy or with unexpected potholes. The water should be fairly shallow during your first sessions, so if using a water complex, make sure you know where the shallow end is.

Finding a safe, controlled environment will make it easier to be successful, but make sure you also set plenty of time aside so there is no rush to get finished. It's also a much nicer experience for your horse if you choose a warm day: boot him up all round, including overreach boots as he may be clumsy or adopt an extravagant action in the water.

A lead from a more confident horse can help boost the confidence of an anxious or inexperienced one. (Courtesy RAD Photographic)

Take Things Steadily

Go equipped with everything you'll need – including food, a friend and your welly boots. Ride your horse up to the edge of the water, being positive but not aggressive or using forceful tactics: you may be able to bully some horses into going in, but they'll never be really confident about it, and others may react violently to such an approach. If you've done some confidence training (*see* page 87, Confidence Training) as part of your preparation, even though your horse may be hesitant, he may nevertheless be prepared to trust you and walk in. If not, you can try dismounting, donning your wellies and leading him in; be careful as some may suddenly launch themselves in from the edge, while others will try and step in your very footprints.

If he likes his food, use this to help tempt him in if he's still inclined to hang back: reward him with some food after each step forward. Very often an apprehensive horse is most likely to follow the example of another, which is where the help of a friend with an ultra confident and reliable horse is invaluable, to give you a lead.

Always let an inexperienced or nervous horse take its time going into water: one foot at a time is fine. Once in, praise him and allow him to stand for a moment or two before walking him forwards so he can get used to the feel of the water moving against his legs. Allow him to sniff at it if he wants, but should he start pawing with a front foot, be careful as he may be thinking about rolling (*see* page 156, Rolling).

Walk him out, and then in and out again a couple of times. He should be less hesitant each time he enters – and that will be quite enough for the first session. If he has a good experience each time he goes in the water he will soon start to feel good about it. Equally, if he forms unpleasant associations because you get cross with him, kicking or yanking at the reins, he is unlikely ever to become willing or reliable about entering water.

During further sessions you can practise walking in and out without a lead as well as with one, and as confidence develops, try a gentle jog which will splash the water about more, and going into deeper parts. Don't ask your horse to move fast, as water resistance will create drag on his front legs, which can result in him losing his balance and falling.

Further Practice

When your horse is relaxed and confident about going into water, use every opportunity to help maintain his new-found assurance, whether splashing through puddles or streams or revisiting a cross-country course water complex from time to time. Do be careful about going into any water you don't know, however: river banks can give way as you are going up or down them, and if you can't see the bottom, lead your horse through, unless it's a well known or indicated crossing point for horses, as there may be potentially injurious objects hidden beneath the surface, or potholes or an unexpectedly steep or boggy bottom. (*See also* page 122, Beach Rides.)

DITCHES

If a ditch is little more than a dip in the ground, crossing it shouldn't pose much of a problem.

BLUE-GREEN ALGAE

Allowing your horse to drink from streams and other water sources is fine if you know the water is clean and uncontaminated, but take care during the summer months when blue-green algae can become a hazard following a spell of hot, dry weather which stimulates its reproduction. Although most frequently found in ponds, lakes, reservoirs and similar stillwater habitats, it can also occur in slow-moving streams. Some species of blue-green algae are harmless, but others form toxins that can be fatal if ingested.

Simply walk down the slope and up the other side, although if looks dark in the bottom or has water in it, take a handful of mane or hold the neckstrap with one hand just in case your horse unexpectedly decides to jump it.

If it is deep with sheer sides you will need to jump it, and many horses find ditches spooky so you may need to ride with conviction. If narrow you may be able to just step over, but with wider ditches, approach in a steady trot with plenty of impulsion, or from canter if your horse is more experienced. Don't flap at him or rush him, but keep him straight, maintaining your contact and looking ahead. Don't look down at the ditch as this will increase the likelihood of your horse stopping at the edge of it.

Hold the mane or neckstrap, as your horse may jump considerably bigger and rounder than the width of the ditch justifies. If you haven't jumped before, or if you think the ditch is too wide, or the take-off and/or landing sides look slippery, ride along the edge until you find a safer place to cross. Be prepared to retrace your steps and find another route if you can't cross safely.

5 Hazards

RIDING ON THE ROADS

Apart from motorways, you generally have the right to ride along or cross any public road. Ride with the flow of traffic and keep well in to the edge on undulating sections of road where traffic may not be able to see you until on the crest of the slope. Don't slop along on a long rein, but keep your horse moving forwards into a contact so you have him under proper control the whole time. Keep both hands on the reins at all times unless you are signalling. Don't ride out on roads when visibility is poor; even with hi-vis clothing it's still a risk, and you will be less likely to spot any potential hazards.

TRAFFIC TRAINING

Many horses find tractors and buses frightening, and it can be difficult and dangerous trying to set up positive experiences with them on the road. Contact your local riding club and suggest a 'traffic training' day when a driver and bus or tractor, plus the services of an experienced trainer or teacher, could be hired for a few hours to help in overcoming anxieties, or broadening the experience of youngsters before venturing on to roads.

Motorists

Despite campaigns to increase driver awareness, many have little or no knowledge of how to overtake horses safely, so be prepared for them to behave unexpectedly either out of ignorance or lack of consideration. Use hand signals when necessary to ask drivers to slow down or stop, thank those who do show consideration (see below), and move into a gateway or side road to allow vehicles you think your horse may find frightening to pass at a safe distance.

Try to avoid using roads at the busiest times of day when folk are travelling to and from work or doing the school run, and at lunchtime when the volume of traffic also increases. If your horse is unsafe in traffic, don't take it out on roads, even quiet ones. It's not worth the risk to you, your horse or other road users.

- Allow plenty of room as you pass parked vehicles, even if they appear empty, as someone may suddenly open a door in front of you, or a dog inside may bark as you pass.

Hand Signals

Give clear and accurate signals to ask other motorists to do anything, and to signal your own intended actions. Always check to the front and behind you before signalling to ensure it is safe: wearing light-coloured gloves or using hi-vis covers or patches will help make signals more visible. Never hold your whip in the hand

TOP LEFT: *Please stop (to road user to your rear).*

TOP RIGHT: *Turning right.*

MIDDLE RIGHT: *Please slow down: extend the right arm to the side, and slowly move it up and down.*

BOTTOM LEFT: *Please stop (to road user to your front).*

BOTTOM RIGHT: *Turning left: hold out your arm for at least three seconds to ensure motorists have seen it.*

which is giving the signal, as it may make your horse, or those of others you are riding with, anxious. Giving a signal does not guarantee your safety or that other road users will heed it, so having given it, always check again before taking your intended action.

Acknowledge considerate behaviour shown towards you by raising a hand: if you need to keep both hands on the reins, at least smile and nod your head. If drivers feel they have been appreciated for giving way they are more likely to do so again.

Riding and Road Safety Test

You should know and obey the Highway Code: it's also a good idea to take the BHS Riding and Road Safety Test, as this will help you gain practical as well as theoretical road-riding skills. Supported by the Department for Transport, the test is open to anyone aged twelve years or over. It isn't necessary to own a horse, as many riding schools organize training and tests for pupils.

The test is made up of three parts covering theory, a simulated road test, and riding a genuine road route, and each of the sections must be passed before being allowed to take the next. A minimum of eight hours training taken over a period of time prior to taking the test is recommended: some additional home study will also be required. Whilst some of the principles will be familiar to riders who drive, there are many significant differences when riding. Details of training and further information on the test are available from the BHS (*see* page 170, Further Information). The Pony Club also runs a 'Road Rider' test, which is similar to the first two sections of the BHS Riding and Road Safety Test.

Junctions

At junctions check behind you as well as to the

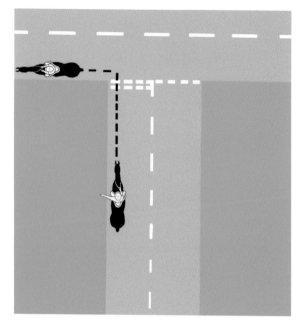

T-junction: minor to major left turn.

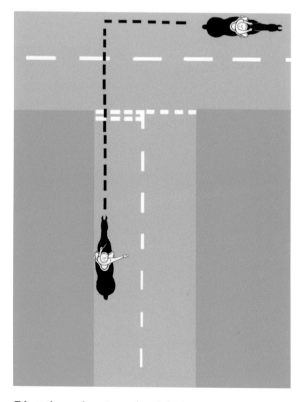

T-junction: minor to major right turn.

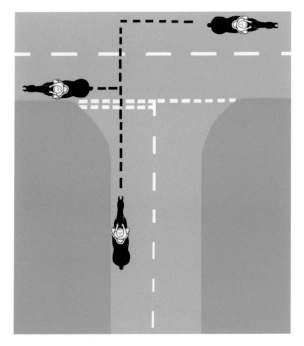

Flared junction showing correct position.

Major road to minor road left turn.

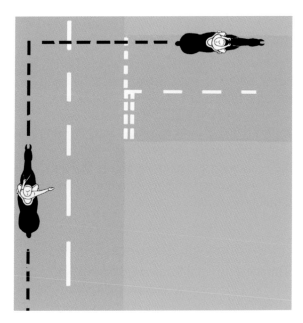

BOTTOM LEFT: *Major road to minor road right turn.*

BOTTOM RIGHT: *Crossroad: keep an eye out for traffic emerging from the opposite junction as well as crossing from left and right in front of you.*

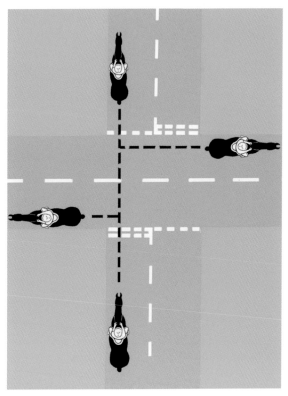

front before giving a clear hand signal indicating that you intend to make a turn: check to rear and front again before actually making your turn. (*See* page 72, Hand Signals.)

Keep to the left side of the road whether you are turning left or right so as to avoid your horse becoming sandwiched between two lines of cars. Halt at 'Give Way' or 'Stop' road markings and check carefully for traffic and that it is safe to continue. When making left turns, check over your left shoulder as well as your right one before moving to ensure you don't have a cyclist that you can't hear passing on your inside.

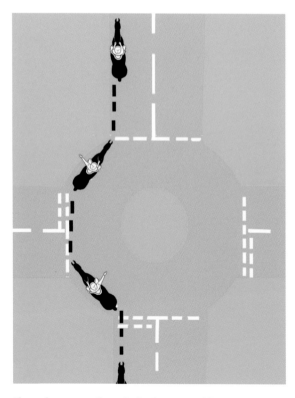

If you have no other choice but to tackle a roundabout, keep to the left. Signal right when crossing exits to indicate that you're not taking it: signal left just before you reach the exit you do want to take. Keep an eye out for vehicles that may cross your path when joining or leaving the roundabout.

Roundabouts

Avoid roundabouts where you can, as drivers need to watch for traffic from many directions, so may be less likely to see you. Consider using the verge or riding along one of the feeder roads until you reach a place where it is safe to cross as a single road as an alternative option.

Busy Road Crossings

Due to insensitive road improvement schemes in the past, there are many places where fast roads cross long-established bridleways and quiet roads. While in legal terms these fast roads do not obstruct horse riders, in practice they can pose a highly dangerous obstruction or hazard. In highly popular areas for riding, improvements have been made at busy road crossings, including increasing sightlines and providing refuge areas and light-controlled crossings.

Only you can judge whether you feel it is safe to cross a particular section of road with your horse, based on your knowledge of him and taking into account your own abilities, the visibility, and the traffic volume and speed. Report difficult and dangerous road crossings to your local council and bridleways officer, so they can be included in any future plans to improve local access opportunities, as and when funding becomes available.

Light-Controlled Crossings

Sometimes special 'Pegasus' crossings are provided for riders as well as cyclists and walkers to use – but even where a light-controlled crossing is intended only for pedestrians, it's worth considering using it, although take care not to put yourself or walkers in danger. If you've had to ride on the pavement to use the crossing, you are technically committing an offence, but you may feel the risk of a rebuke from a pedestrian or police officer a price worth paying to allow you to cross safely.

Traffic Lights

Traffic light signals apply as much to horse riders as to other road users. If you see only an amber light, do not rush forwards in an attempt to beat the red light. Halt at the stop line painted on the road: you can continue only if the amber light appears after you have crossed the stop line.

Approach temporary traffic lights at roadworks with particular care, as they may not control all traffic entering the affected roads, or give enough time for a rider to get past before changing. Cables used to connect the lights (or to operate other equipment) can spook your horse, and he may be reluctant to walk over them. They should be moved or covered so he doesn't damage the cable: if a current is passing through them it could result in a fatal electrical shock. Even if switched off, damage to the protective covering could lead to an accident later. You may need to attract the attention of the workmen to do this. Unless you really have no other option, it's usually best to take an alternative route.

Other Hazards

Motorists are encouraged to read the road ahead, and riders should do exactly the same. Potential road hazards aren't just posed by passing cars, but by a whole host of things such as dustbins and rubbish bags left out for collection, baby buggies, pedestrians with umbrellas or walking dogs, bicycles, plastic traffic cones, discarded wrappers blowing around or children running out from house doorways. These can all cause your horse to be startled and to step sideways into the path of

oncoming traffic unless you are prepared for them. (*See* page 159, Shying and Spooking.)

Some hazards can be almost soundless, so check frequently over your shoulder to ensure you don't get caught out by overtaking cyclists (who may try to pass on the inside) or joggers on pavements.

Roadworks and building sites are generally best avoided as there are likely to be cones, stripy boards, flashing lights, flapping lengths of coloured tape, heavy vehicles and noisy machinery operating, which your horse may find alarming. Potholes, drain covers and road markings can also be frightening for your horse, although you can do much to help him overcome his fears by doing some confidence training (*see* page 87, Confidence Training).

COUNTRYSIDE HAZARDS

Country Roads

Rural roads may have less traffic than in more built-up areas, but vehicles often travel much faster than they should, even where visibility is poor due to narrow, winding and undulating lanes and high hedges. Furthermore the type of vehicles you meet may be frightening for your horse: tractors and other agricultural vehicles are often large and noisy. Use your ears and eyes to warn you of approaching vehicles and note any gateways, verges and other areas where you can take refuge if necessary. If your horse finds farm machinery alarming, it may be helpful to try some traffic training (*see* page 72, Riding on the Roads).

Country roads and lanes are also popular with cyclists, who may spook your horse by passing without warning. Also these minor roads are less likely to be gritted in winter so may be icy, especially in shaded areas, while fallen leaves will stick to the surface of little used roads, making them more slippery in autumn.

The apparent peacefulness of your surroundings can lull you into a sense of false security. How many potential hazards can you spot in this seemingly quiet country lane? (The answers are below: cover them up until you have noted down the ones you can see, then uncover them to see how many you have missed!)

Answers:

1. Washing hanging out: it may flap unexpectedly in the wind.
2. Dog run and kennel: the unseen dog may suddenly run out and bark.
3. Wheelie bin: some horses find these especially unnerving.
4. Unattended wheelbarrow: a person might appear unexpectedly from the vegetation nearby.
5. Change of surface colour across the road: this may distract a horse or make him hesitant.
6. The front door of the cottage opens straight on to the road, as do the dormer windows: any sudden noise or movement associated with these may startle your horse.
7. 60mph road sign: cars may be travelling at speed.
8. The narrow single-track road allows little space for vehicles to overtake safely.
9. The bend in the road ahead gives limited visibility of oncoming traffic.

On narrow roads be ready to stop traffic behind you if other cars are approaching and there isn't enough room for you to be passed at a safe distance. Once the driver has seen you, calmly take up a position to the centre of your lane to remove any temptation for the driver to try and squeeze past. Acknowledge their presence with a wave, and use the first passing place or gateway to allow them to pass.

Livestock

You may well have livestock to contend with, either grazing in fields close by your route or through which a bridleway passes, or being driven across or along country lanes. Give them as wide a berth as possible and use a shoulder-in or shoulder-fore position (*see* page 118, Schooling) to help you maintain control. Remain in walk so you do not excite the livestock into running around and alarming your horse. When riding through fields with stock in, always take especial care not to come between bulls with cows, or between cows with calves, as they may be highly protective and therefore aggressive.

Many horses are also anxious about passing near pigs; the company of a steady escort horse can help boost the confidence of one that is concerned about these or any other farm animals.

Don't let your horse approach equines in adjacent fields which may follow you, whinnying as you ride past. Apart from not knowing the health status of such animals, close contact can lead to dangerous reactions such as striking out with the forefeet or rearing.

Stock in fields you want to pass through can be a nuisance if they gather round as you try to open or shut the gate to get through. Some will move away if you wave your arms at them or shout, but take care you don't scare your horse, too. Take an alternative route if your horse can't cope with stock crowding round.

In some areas your route may pass through open country where semi-wild horses are grazing (such as the New Forest) or fields where domesticated horses are kept. Do always consider whether it's better to avoid the situation, and remember that sexual hormones can make this more problematic at certain times of the year. Loose horses may seek to interact in all sorts of ways with your horse. Similarly, stallions are sometimes kept in fields through which bridleways pass, and need to be treated with caution.

Barbed wire and electric fencing are commonly used to help keep livestock contained: be careful if riding alongside, as wire can inflict unpleasant wounds and electric fencing can give your horse a nasty shock should he brush too close. Some horses are also very sensitive to the rhythmic ticking noise of an electric fence energizer, or from a faulty or damp section of fencing as the electricity sparks down to the ground (*see* page 54, Obstructions).

noise can carry some distance, and even when shooting is not taking place, pheasants may startle your horse by flying out noisily from immediately under his feet.

Public rights of way remain open even if shooting is taking place, but there is no general legal obligation for land managers to advise the public as to when it will be happening, and although there are legal restrictions on shooting near public roads, landowners are quite entitled to shoot from or across public rights of way. The landowner does have a responsibility to make sure you are not obstructed or put in danger, but you can help avoid any potentially dangerous situations by sticking to designated paths, wearing hi-vis garments, and heeding warning signs. You can also check with the gamekeeper or estate office as to the dates of their shoots so you can plan an alternative route if your horse is liable to be frightened.

Sometimes shooting occurs without the permission of the landowner, particularly around dawn and dusk and at weekends. As the people involved are breaking the law when doing this, they are unlikely to have much regard for the safety of other people; they may also have loose dogs with them, to retrieve their spoils or chase rabbits and hares. This is another good reason for wearing high visibility clothing even when not on the road.

Shooting

The loud bang of a shotgun may be heard at any time, because although there are specific seasons for shooting different types of game, these seasons have a range of different dates; furthermore animals classed as 'pests' – rabbits, pigeons, magpies and crows – can be shot at any time of year, day or night. Also the 'swish' noise from rifles used for shooting rabbits and deer, although less common and quieter, can be very unsettling to horses. In certain areas the

Bird Scarers

Farmers should not locate a gas-powered bird scarer that sounds like the shot from a shotgun near to a public right of way or any other access route, especially those used by horses, but sometimes it is impractical to locate them where they won't be heard by passing riders. However, as some go off at regular intervals throughout the day, it is possible to predict when the next bang will happen so you can avoid being close to it, or at least be prepared.

- In Scotland many deerstalking estates participate in the hill phones service, which allows you to check if stalking is taking place and to change your route accordingly. A map-based website is also being tried: *see* Further Information.

Silage Wrap and Bags

Plastic bags are particularly liable to spook horses: even if motionless as you approach, a sudden change in wind strength or direction can cause them to flap suddenly or move towards you. You may well come across such 'monsters' near wrapped bales of silage and other farm products, where sections of wrap are frequently torn off or simply flap from the end of a bale.

Military Aircraft

In some areas, low-flying military jets, transport planes and helicopters pose a particular hazard, especially in the more remote parts of the United Kingdom. Horses living in these areas become accustomed to the noise, but it can be a problem if riding your horse away from home or on holiday in these places. The Ministry of Defence does publish details on its website of when low-flying exercises are planned to take place; you can also obtain information by contacting the MoD Freephone Helpline.

If you have a fall and become separated from your horse when riding along a route that passes through a training area, you should not leave the route in pursuit of him, but must contact local MoD staff, otherwise you could both be at risk of injury or death if you were to wander into exclusion or danger areas. (*See* page 170, Further Information.)

Air ambulances and police helicopters may also fly low; making yourself as conspicuous as possible by wearing hi-vis clothing (especially

an exercise sheet) will help them to spot you up to half a mile sooner than otherwise, and to take evasive action.

Wind Turbines

Wind turbines are an increasingly common feature in the countryside, both close to farms and on more exposed, hilly ground. The blade movement and the noise can spook your horse, and changes in wind direction and speed can dramatically change how he perceives these from one day to the next. However, horses generally learn that there is nothing to fear if introduced to them in a calm manner, with the help if necessary of a steady escort horse.

Ticks

Ticks are blood-sucking parasites that attach themselves to you or your horse and swell to the size of a pea as they suck up your blood. In most cases this is just unpleasant, but as ticks can carry life-threatening diseases they should be taken seriously.

They are most commonly found in tall vegetation such as long grass, bracken, bushes and woodland, especially where sheep and deer live. Prevention is better than cure, so cover any exposed flesh on yourself. Check for ticks on finishing your ride if you've been in an area

---

NOTES FOR RIDE LEADERS

Even though a horse may be accustomed to livestock, sometimes clients have a fear of cattle and other animals. Be prepared to respond to this in a calm, professional way, and adapt your route if necessary.

where they are known to be present. Remove any you find using a special tick hook, following the instructions provided. If you feel unwell in the days or weeks after being bitten by a tick, consult your doctor, as tick-related infections are sometimes overlooked. (*See* page 170, Further Information.)

BARRIERS

Cattlegrids

A cattlegrid should have a side gate, with a barrier positioned between it and the grid to allow horses to bypass it safely, without inadvertently stepping on it and getting a foot trapped in the gaps. Nevertheless, always take great care with such obstacles: always approach slowly, and be aware that if your horse spooks or tries to bolt, he may try and go straight across it. Unless you are sure you can readily open, get through and close the bypass gate

from horseback, it's safer to dismount and lead your horse through, positioning yourself between him and the grid.

If you are riding with others, allow the most fidgety horse to pass through first, and the quietest to bring up the rear, as not all horses will queue quietly: if one becomes anxious about being left behind, it may try to rush through the gap where the cattlegrid is. (*See also* page 169, Trapped in a Cattlegrid.)

The bypass gate is often within a few inches of the metal grid itself, which can make an alarming noise when cars go over it. It may therefore be advisable either to wait until there is no traffic, or to ask motorists to stop while you negotiate the gate.

Horse Stiles

Horse stiles usually consist of one or two or more parallel sleepers or raised rails; they are installed to deter illegal motorcycle use. They

Horse stile.

should not pose a problem to horses, although you should stay in walk so your horse doesn't try to jump them. Practising over poles at home will ensure your horse is confident about stepping over such barriers (*see also* page 162, Stumbling).

Level Crossings

You may encounter a level crossing where a road or bridleway crosses a railway line; check the rail timetables to find out when scheduled trains are due so you can avoid them whenever possible. Flashing lights, barriers moving up or down and audible warning signals can be just as alarming for horses as the sight and sound of a train flashing past, so if you have to wait, move to a safe distance away, and only proceed when all other traffic has crossed.

Take particular care at crossings where there are no barriers: look and listen to make sure the track is clear; if there are barriers, wait for them to be fully raised before crossing. Should the red lights keep flashing after the train has passed, continue to wait a safe distance away as it means another one will be along soon. At some crossings you may be required to dismount where a 'horse riders dismount' sign is displayed.

When it's safe to cross, your horse may be concerned about the change in surface: look ahead to the far side and ride forwards positively. If you have done some confidence training with him (*see* page 87, Confidence Training) he will be more likely to take it all in his stride.

GATES

Always leave a gate as you find it: if it is closed, be sure to leave it securely fastened behind you. Opening (and shutting) a gate while mounted is easier and safer if your horse understands

what you want him to do. The simplest way to teach him is to start by leading him in hand. Once he has learned how to organize his body while being led, it will be easier for him to repeat the manoeuvre with you in the saddle.

Keep yourself between your horse and the gate so you can prevent it from swinging back on to him. This may mean that you'll be leading from the off (right) side rather than the near side, and if he is not very good at this, teach it to him first.

Open the gate wide enough so that you can both walk through without risk of your horse catching his hips or sides on the gatepost or any protruding catches.

Once you are safely through the gate, turn your horse to face it while you close it again. Repeat from the other side, so he is used to the gate opening both away from him and towards him.

When he is easy to manoeuvre in hand, try the same thing while mounted. Begin by opening the gate away from you both: stand him parallel to the gate with his head just past the latch, and put your whip and reins into the hand furthest away from it. Reach out with your other hand and push the gate open: it will help if your horse knows how to do a turn on the forehand and has learned some leg yield (*see* page 116, Schooling) as he will be easier to position.

Again, make sure you open the gate wide enough for you both to pass through comfortably, keeping well clear of the gatepost and latch: he will not make allowances for your legs on each side of his body.

When he is confident doing this, teach him how to open the gate towards him, which is much trickier.

Safe Procedures

If you are riding with other riders, decide whether each rider will catch the gate as they

Take care when going through gateways as wet as this one, in case your horse tries to avoid the puddles and boggy patches and gets too close to the gatepost.

pass through, or – the safest option – if one person will hold it open while everyone goes through.

Take care with self-closing gates as they can startle your horse if they swing against his hindquarters before you are all the way through.

Make sure your reins are short enough before you start, and take care that martingales and reins don't get caught on latches.

You may need to dismount to deal with sagging or awkwardly sited gates. Cross your stirrups over your horse's shoulders in front of the saddle so there is no danger of them swinging and getting snagged on the gate latch as you lead your horse through.

Don't lengthen your nearside stirrup too much to remount; if overlong your left foot may swing under your horse's belly, or you may not be able to clear the back of the saddle with your right leg. Look around for something to give you more height such as a log or sloping ground.

Teach your horse to stand quietly alongside a gate, so that if sturdy enough, you can use it to mount from. Try if possible to mount from the hinged end of the gate, as this is the strongest part.

Narrow Spaces Exercise

Some horses have issues about passing through gateways and other narrow spaces, often because they have caught their hips on the posts, or because doors or gates have swung shut on them when they were only halfway through. These horses may be reluctant to go through any sort of narrow passageway, and when they do will often rush, increasing the risk of injury.

It is worthwhile spending time at home helping such a horse to overcome his concerns. The following TTEAM exercise will also help prepare him for other possible obstacles he may have to negotiate, such as narrow bridges and underpasses.

● Create a 'wall' with stacked hay or straw bales, or by setting up a jump pole at waist height between two jump stands with blankets or rugs hung over it to make a more solid-looking barrier.
● Walk your horse in hand past this barrier, keeping yourself between him and it, so that if he moves to the side away from it he won't trample on you. Allow him to pass it at a distance he finds 'safe', and let him look at and inspect it if he wants.
● Ask him to halt just before the barrier, while level with it, and just after it, to encourage

him to slow down and think about what he is doing, rather than panicking and rushing.

- Once confident enough to walk past in close proximity, introduce a similar barrier on the other side, with a good distance between them. Walk into the wide tunnel formed by the two sides, stop in the centre and then walk on again to the end. Some horses may find it hard to stop at first, in which case make the distance wider and keep walking through until he is relaxed enough to be able to stop.

- As his confidence grows – which may take many sessions over a period of days or even weeks if he has a high level of concern – gradually start closing up the distance until he's walking calmly through the tunnel with it close on each side.

- Stay level with his head rather than his shoulder while leading him, as you have more control in this position, and keep to the side so that if he tries to rush forwards you don't get knocked over. If he does try to rush, you have taken things too fast.

- When he is unperturbed about doing the exercise in hand, try it while mounted, but run through the same complete sequence of steps, with a single 'wall' initially before adding a second side to form a 'tunnel'.

- Teaching the TTEAM Sliding Saddlecloth exercise (*see* page 144) can also be very helpful as it teaches your horse not to worry about things touching his sides.

Locked Gates

Like any other obstruction on a public right of way, a locked gate is unlawful and should be reported. Check first, however, in case a padlock and chain can be unhooked on the other side.

If a gate is locked on a permitted path there is usually a good reason, such as temporary closure for farming activities, or to stop usage

NOTES FOR RIDE ESCORTS

A chore for you can be an enjoyable achievement for a client; thus gate opening can be a great opportunity for more experienced riders to put into practical use some of the skills learnt in the school. Always check the gate is properly shut after a client has finished – you are responsible.

Make sure the rest of the ride waits in a safe and orderly way while the gate is being opened. Explain to them that it's important they come through in single file, and to keep clear of both sides. Hold open gates that are liable to swing shut while they pass through.

Should it be necessary to dismount to open or shut a gate, ride escorts should be agile enough and suitably mounted as to be able to remount from the ground if necessary.

by people who haven't paid; contact the landowner to clarify the situation.

In some cases you may find the local council has inadvertently installed narrow gates or barriers to prevent unauthorized use by motor vehicles, without realizing that these can also obstruct horse riders. These don't become lawful simply because the council put them in; report these too, as there are ways to restrict unauthorized access without interfering with the right to ride.

BRIDGES AND UNDERPASSES

Bridges that are narrow or have surfaces that are noisy can cause horses to be anxious: confidence training (see page 89) and practising the TTEAM narrow spaces exercise can be helpful.

Take especial care when riding across bridges over rivers as the surfaces are likely to be slippery in winter; if the footing is uncertain, dismount and lead your horse. Unusual and unexpected sights such as kayaks in the river may also startle your horse; and watch out for anglers, because the sound of a fishing line being cast can sound like the swish of a lunge whip.

Bridges that cross over roads can also be daunting, and it's sensible to introduce your horse to such hazards in the company of a steady and experienced horse. Although modern road bridges are generally better designed these days, there are still many with low railings and open parapets that present a real danger to riders if thrown, and also make the traffic passing underneath far more visible to your horse than need be. On bridges where

there is a known danger or history of accidents, you may well see a sign requesting riders to dismount. Always heed these warnings, and don't be afraid to dismount in other situations – or simply turn back if you feel you can't cross in safety.

If riding over or under a railway line, find out scheduled train times so you can try to avoid them, but as they don't always run to time, use your ears as you get closer, and also look for any nearby signals – when set to green, a train may well be expected and likely to pass quickly.

Underpasses beneath busy roads can be equally challenging; as well as having to go into a confined space, it may be dimly lit and with spooky echoes that magnify sounds. The horse's eyes will adjust more slowly to low light conditions than yours, so he may hesitate

In many cases horses are expected to ford rivers – a bridge like this could be too weak and thus dangerous for horses. (Courtesy RAD Photographic)

initially. Allow him time for his eyes to become accustomed, and speak reassuringly to him – impatience or coercion is likely to make him more anxious. He may be more confident if you dismount and lead him: you will need to do this anyway if there isn't much headroom.

In many cases horses are expected to ford rivers, as the adjacent narrow bridges are there to keep walkers' feet dry – this sort of bridge may be fine for walkers and cyclists, but could be too weak and thus dangerous for horses. If you are not sure about a bridge, ford the river if you can do so safely. Alternatively dismount, tie up your horse, and inspect it on foot: lead your horse if you feel it is safe to do so, or find an alternative route if not. Cross the stirrups over the saddle, or run them up so they don't get caught on anything, rather than leaving them dangling.

CONFIDENCE TRAINING

Spending time at home doing some confidence training with your horse is time well spent: by improving his balance, surefootedness and spatial awareness, and increasing his self-assurance, he will be a safer and more relaxed ride on varying terrains and in different situations.

You can set up many different exercises at home, introducing new sights, sounds and experiences in a safe environment, thereby accustoming him to objects he may meet when he is out and about (see page 72, Riding on the Roads, and page 21, Introducing Young Horses to Hacking). Keep calm and allow him to stay at a distance he considers safe (see page 159, Shying and Spooking), only moving closer as he becomes less anxious and more trusting of your judgment. As his boldness increases try moving your 'hazards' to different locations so they don't become associated with a single spot and he learns not to be concerned, wherever they are.

TTEAM Work

TTEAM exercises such as the narrow spaces exercise (see page 84), the single pole exercise (see page 163), and sliding saddlecloth (see page 144) and walking over a variety of different surfaces can be of huge benefit in developing psychological as well as physical poise, and good preparation for dealing with obstacles you might need to negotiate out hacking, such as bridges, drain covers, tree roots, uneven ground and road markings. Equally importantly, they encourage your horse to participate in the learning process instead of simply being programmed with a series of set responses to certain prompts. This means that whenever anything occurs which he hasn't encountered before he'll be more confident and better equipped to work out what to do, and less likely to have a panic reaction.

Of course it helps if the rider or handler is calm and confident too: sometimes human anxieties need to be addressed as well as those of the horse, otherwise you will tend to keep setting each other off (see page 16, Hacking Nerves).

TTEAM Plastic Sheeting Exercise

Plastic sheeting is used here, but try other surfaces too, such as a sheet of heavy duty plywood, tarpaulin, rubber matting, flattened cardboard boxes or carpeting: these will all produce different noises and feels underfoot when your horse stands on them, as well as looking unusual. This can help make him more self-assured when dealing with new and different surfaces you may encounter out hacking.

Always teach this exercise in hand before trying it mounted; and although the handlers in the photos aren't wearing hard hats or gloves, it is recommended that you do so. While leading your horse, stay level with his head rather than his shoulder, as this will give you more control.

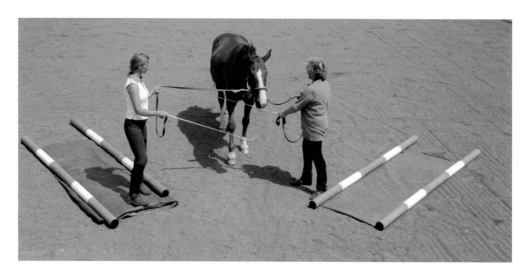

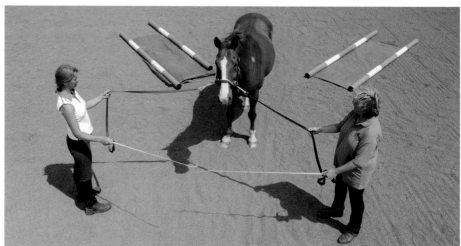

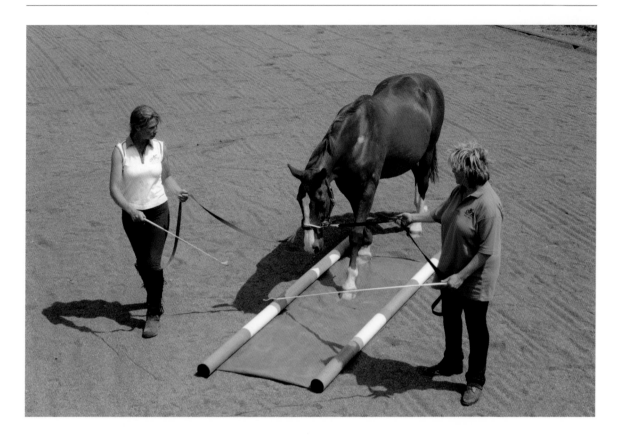

Attach your leadrein to the side ring of the headcollar noseband as this lessens pressure on the poll, which can cause your horse to carry his head high and to be reluctant to move freely forwards.

If you have a friend who can help, you can lead the horse with one of you on each side, as shown in the pictures, as this will make it easier to keep him straight; the long white dressage whips (wands) are also used to help guide and contain him (*see* page 162, Stumbling). Keep the leadreins as free of tension as possible. You as handler should give all the signals to slow, stop and move forwards while your assistant takes a passive role, not giving any signals, but helping to keep your horse balanced and central between you by taking up a contact if you ask them to. As they do, you will need to yield a little so you don't end up wrestling with each other. This leading position does require

good communication between you both, so should be practised before trying the following exercise, but once mastered, it helps develop self carriage and self control in your horse; furthermore if he is slightly nervous not only is it a very safe way to lead, but one which promotes confidence.

- Set out two pieces of plastic sheeting in a V shape with a gap of around 3m (10ft) in the middle between the two ends. If your horse is very nervous, you may need to move them even further apart. Make sure it is weighed down so it doesn't blow about. If working on your own, use just one piece of plastic which you can walk past, progressively moving closer: keep yourself between it and your horse so that if he spooks at it he'll be moving away from you, rather than on top of you.

- Walk around the outside of the V, and if your horse walks quietly past it, try walking into the arms of the V, halting just before, and just after going through the gap. This teaches him to wait, and to look and listen to you whenever he is in a potentially frightening situation. If he tries to rush through the gap you may be asking too much of him too soon, so move the ends of the plastic further apart until he is more comfortable about it. Very nervous horses may find it hard to halt with the surface behind them – this will give you a better understanding as to his confidence levels – but don't force him to stop. If he continually has to keep moving forwards after going through the gap in the plastic, go back a step.
- As he becomes more confident, gradually begin moving the ends of the plastic closer together so the gap in the middle becomes smaller. As this happens, begin stepping on it yourself with first one, and then both feet so your horse becomes accustomed to the noise.
- When he is unconcerned about this, bring both ends of the plastic together and ask your horse to step on to it. If he wants to inspect it first, that's fine – you can even put some food on it to encourage him to put his nose down and check it out. Do not, however, allow him to mouth it, because if he picks up the sheeting with his teeth he may panic and shoot backwards still holding it: this reflex action means that he will keep his teeth clenched and won't let go, and this could cause a serious accident.
- Once he is calmly walking on to and over the plastic, try walking across both arms of the V; and when he is taking this in his stride, try it along the length of one of the pieces of plastic.
- Once he has reached this stage you can try it while mounted; repeat each of the stages above.

- Don't try and complete all this work during one session, but spread it out over several days or weeks, depending on your horse's level of concern.
- Don't attempt to move the sheeting while also holding your horse: either ask your assistant to hold him, or if you are on your own, tie him at a safe distance away.

CLICKER TRAINING

Clicker training was originally devised as a way of training dolphins and has since become very popular with dog trainers; it has also been used with great success with horses. Moreover it can be useful in helping overcome anxieties about scary objects by positively rewarding those behaviours, such as calmness, which you want your horse to repeat.

A clicker is a small plastic box with a metal tongue inside which, when pressed down with a thumb, makes a distinctive clicking noise. However, you can use any noise as long as it's distinctly different, precise and consistent. Making a 'click' noise with your tongue can be a useful alternative as it leaves both hands free – thus you can readily 'click' your horse when mounted.

The noise is associated with a food reward, so that when your horse hears it, he knows that whatever he was doing at that precise moment was something you liked, and promises that a reward will follow. This then encourages him to repeat the action in order to earn another reward.

Although the principles are fairly simple, they are often misunderstood, so it can be a good idea to ask an experienced clicker trainer to help you get started (*see* page 170, Further Information).

6 Weather

RIDING IN HOT WEATHER

Better weather and longer daylight hours during the warmer months of the year allow more time for riding, but it's not without a few discomforts and inconveniences for you as well as your horse. In hot weather it is advisable to be prepared in the following ways:

- You should always wear your riding hat, but may find a lightweight one with ventilation holes to aid air circulation more comfortable.

- Wear light, loose-fitting clothing that will allow perspiration to evaporate. A long-sleeved shirt will prevent the shoulders from getting sunburnt and will offer less bare flesh for midges, mosquitoes and other biting insects to feast on.
- Wear safety-type sunglasses to protect your eyes from the sun's glare.
- Apply high factor sunscreen to all areas of exposed skin.
- Carry a pack of travel-size wet wipes – they can be very refreshing.

Ride later in the day when it's cooler – but don't get caught out miles from home as dusk falls. (Courtesy RAD Photographic)

- Dehydration can affect you as well as your horse: on longer rides carry a drink for yourself and sip at it frequently, even if you don't feel thirsty. You can buy special bottle holders that attach to your saddle – some will even keep drinks cool.
- If the opportunity arises during your ride, run cool water over your wrists for ten seconds as this can help reduce your core body temperature; the effect can last up to one hour.
- Use insect repellents: impregnated wipes are useful for areas where sprays are difficult to apply, such as the face and neck. You can also pin one to your hat cover if you wear a skull cap. If planning a riding holiday in Scotland, be aware that midges in affected areas are often worse in late summer.
- Carry a pocket-size bite and sting spray. If you have had a severe allergic response to stings in the past make sure you are wearing medical ID of some kind (*see* page 28, What to Wear) and have any emergency medication prescribed by your GP with you.
- Know the signs of heat exhaustion and heat stroke, and what to do (*see*, page 94).

SUMMER HORSE CARE

Similar problems affect horses as riders during the summer months. When experiencing an unaccustomed heatwave bear in mind that it can take at least ten days for a horse to acclimatize to higher humidity and temperatures. Ride during the cooler parts of the day, take things more steadily, and provide opportunities for him to drink along the way.

Sunburn

Sparsely haired and unpigmented areas of skin can be vulnerable to sunburn. Protect white or pink muzzles with either a veterinary sunblock or a human hypoallergenic one: always try a small test patch first. If the skin does become burned it will appear inflamed and be tender to the touch: should it become blistered or oozy, get veterinary attention.

Dehydration

Nearly 70 per cent of your horse's bodyweight is made up of water. Generally he is able to replace any lost fluids through drinking, but during hot, humid conditions or if he sweats heavily he may lose more than he takes on and is potentially at risk of becoming dehydrated. If severe, dehydration can be fatal: it also predisposes to heat exhaustion and heat stroke.

Symptoms of Dehydration

Keep an eye out for signs of dehydration – they may be hard to spot in the early stages, but in hot weather you should be aware of any such changes in your horse. Watch out for the following symptoms:

- He may become dull or lethargic.
- Urination becomes infrequent or ceases: if the urine is becoming darker in colour this may indicate the onset of dehydration.
- The gums will become dry or tacky.
- He will develop a weak, fast pulse.
- Sunken eyes.
- Brick-red mucous membranes.
- Cool extremities.

You can also use the pinch and capillary refill tests to check if a horse is dehydrated.

Pinch test: If the skin at the base of the neck just in front of the shoulder is pinched up between finger and thumb it should return to its flat appearance immediately when released. If the skin takes longer than two seconds to flatten, your horse is dehydrated, and the

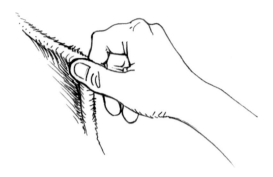

The pinch test.

content than hay, or soaking the hay. Feeds can also be made wetter.

- Consult your vet or an equine nutritionist as to whether your horse would benefit from added salt in his diet or electrolyte supplements. Allow free access to a salt lick in the field or stable.

longer it takes to go flat, the more severe the problem.

Capillary refill test: Lift the lip and press the gum firmly with the ball of your thumb or finger. This will leave a white mark, which should return to pink within two seconds when the pressure is released. If it takes longer than this, your horse is suffering from dehydration (or shock): again, the longer it takes, the more severe the problem.

Preventing Dehydration

The following are ways that will help to prevent dehydration:

- Choose cooler times of day, and shady areas such as woodland to ride in if possible.
- Cool your horse off after rides by sponging him down with cool water. This will reduce sweating and therefore dehydration.
- Fat, unfit or thick-coated horses are most at risk, so attend to diet, do not overstress the horse, and consider clipping during the summer months as well as in the winter.
- The gut can act as a reservoir for fluids, so increase water intake by giving either haylage, which has a higher moisture

Allow your horse to drink at every opportunity out on rides, although be careful to use uncontaminated sources. Ensure that fresh clean water is always available to your horse at home. (Courtesy RAD Photographic)

If you think your horse is dehydrated you should do the following:

- Stop work and lead him to a shady area.
- Sponge him down.
- Offer frequent drinks of water.

If he is severely dehydrated, or if he won't drink, call your vet as it may be necessary to administer fluids intravenously.

Heatstroke and Heat Exhaustion

Dehydration can lead to heat exhaustion and heatstroke, potentially fatal conditions usually seen in horses that are overexerted in hot, humid weather. The horse may sweat profusely initially, but as he begins to dehydrate, his body temperature may rise dangerously high. Heart and respiratory rates also increase, and the skin will feel hot but dry as he loses the ability to cool himself through sweating; he may appear listless and uncoordinated.

- Stop work immediately, call the vet, and begin emergency cooling while waiting for him to arrive: move the horse to a shady area, preferably where there is a breeze, or use a fan if one is available; keep hosing and sponging down with cool water, and offer frequent drinks. Prevention is always the best policy: follow the same guidelines as for preventing dehydration.

Flies

Flies and other biting insects can make hacking out miserable for your horse. Some have an extremely painful bite, others can cause eye infections and ear plaques, and a certain type of midge is responsible for the intensely itchy and distressing condition known as sweet itch. These midges occur most prolifically in wet areas such as lakes and streams, and are also dense in wooded, shady areas – all places where you might choose to ride on warm days, but which are best avoided if you have a horse that suffers from this condition. They are most active at dawn and dusk – approximately between 4pm and 8am – so try to plan your rides for different times of the day.

Sweaty, smelly and dirty horses are more attractive to flies, so on warm days wash off your horse after your ride. This is also easier and quicker for you and more comfortable for him than brushing the sweat off when it is dry.

ELECTROLYTE LOSS

When your horse sweats, he also loses electrolytes (or body salts), which are vital for various bodily functions. These are normally supplied through the diet, but excessive sweating can lead to electrolyte deficiencies which may be manifested by a condition known as the 'thumps' – spasmodic twitching of the flanks with an audible noise. Call your vet, who will be able to administer appropriate intravenous treatment to remedy the problem.

Fly cap.

Physical insect deterrents include fly fringes and caps with earpieces – the sort with tassels are best, as the movement will help keep flies away from the eyes. It is also possible to buy fly veils similar to those used for turnout, which the manufacturer claims do not impair vision, and mesh fly sheets designed for riding in, which cover most of the horse and can be useful if flies are a real nuisance.

A wide selection of commercial preparations with insect-repelling properties can be bought as sprays, creams, gels, wipes and roll-ons; for added protection wrap a wipe around the browband. Many people also swear by 'natural' repellents, including adding garlic or cider vinegar to the feed, and wiping vinegar over the coat. The length of time that repellents are effective varies, and they may need to be reapplied frequently: take a roll-on, wipes or other similarly easily carried products so you can apply a top-up as necessary.

● If your horse has a long, full mane, plait it into pigtails or a running plait along the crest to keep it off the neck to help keep your horse cooler.

COPING WITH ADVERSE WEATHER CONDITIONS

Even though the weather may look settled, in some areas it can change rapidly and with little warning. Checking the daily forecasts will help

Weather conditions can change rapidly in some areas, so be prepared to change your plans and cut your ride short, especially if visibility begins to deteriorate. (Courtesy RAD Photographic)

you know what to be prepared for, so you can dress yourself and your horse appropriately – or in the case of a severe weather warning, to change your plans.

There is an excellent free website for riders, which gives accurate, very localized forecasts for the coming week at three-hour intervals across the UK and many other countries (*see* Further Information).

Weather Warnings

Severe weather warnings are usually well publicized on the television and radio, and you can also find out what's happening in your area on the internet. After a spell of bad weather you may still need to exercise care: for example, storms and gales may have left fallen trees and power lines.

When weather conditions become extreme, don't be a martyr to riding out. You will probably both be miserable, as your horse is unlikely to enjoy it either, and you could be putting yourselves both at risk. If you absolutely must exercise your horse, find an alternative such as hiring an indoor school.

Fog

Fog can be as potentially dangerous when you are riding over familiar ground as it can in unknown territory; it can be very disorienting, and it is easy to miss turnings and landmarks. Fog can also affect your own visibility; hi-vis clothing helps, but when fog is dense, motorists may not see you soon enough to take evasive action. It can also muffle sound, making it harder for you to hear approaching vehicles, or deceiving you as to how close they are.

If visibility is obviously deteriorating, head for home immediately, or at least to somewhere you can safely wait until the weather clears. Should you get caught out in it, it may be safer to dismount and lead your horse so you can carefully check the ground ahead: it will also be easier to see the track you are following, and therefore to remain on it. If you are in an isolated area with hazards such as cliff edges or bogs, stay put until you can see where you are going rather than risk wandering out of your way and stumbling into danger.

If people are likely to be out searching for you, blow your whistle to help them locate you (*see* page 148, Lost). Letting your horse pick his own way in the hope that he will find his way home is not generally a sensible idea, as he is as likely to go the wrong way as the right way.

Rain

Rain can make grass and the surface of structures you may need to cross, such as bridges or ramps made of wood, very slippery. Driving rain can cause poor visibility for both you and motorists, and in some areas even quite short periods of intense rainfall can lead to flash floods. Keep to higher ground and out of dry streambeds and gullies, and don't cross streams already swollen by floodwater and beginning to flow more strongly: fast-flowing water can readily unbalance your horse and sweep him off his feet, even when it is quite shallow. There is also the risk of being struck and injured by rubbish and debris that is being carried along, above or below the surface (*see also* page 69, Water).

The metal covers of underground culverts and drains in road surfaces can be blown out by floods, and a seemingly innocent-looking shallow puddle might in fact be the exit point for a deep, uncovered inspection shaft, with the concomitant potential for breaking your horse's leg. So keep out of puddles, and if the full width of the road is flooded and you have no alternative but to go through, dismount and carefully lead your horse, sliding your feet forwards in turn to check for any uncovered holes.

Even when the rain has stopped it can still be a hazard: bright sunshine reflecting off a wet road surface can often dazzle motorists, who may not see you until they are very close.

Freezing Conditions

Icy patches aren't always easy to spot, and even on sunny days may not melt in shady areas, so always take special care if there has been a hard frost or a spell of freezing weather (*see* page 63, Slippery Surfaces). The road surfaces of bridges are especially prone to freezing, long before other surfaces. The ground will also be very hard, and if frozen in ruts and ridges may affect your horse's footing, or cause bruising.

In cold weather your horse may be a little more on his toes, so if necessary work him for a short while in the school before going out. If he is clipped, an exercise sheet may be required.

Wind

Windy weather always makes it feel much colder, as well as causing greater heat loss: if using an exercise blanket ensure it has a fillet string to keep it in place and prevent it from being blown upwards. Blowy days can cause even normally sensible horses to be a little skittish, so be alert for objects being blown around which may spook him. Don't risk going out in strong winds which may cause man-made structures to collapse or weakened trees to fall.

Hail

Hail can be painful as well as affecting visibility should you get caught out in it. However, hail showers usually last only a short time, so find shelter if possible and wait it out. If you can't

find any, and the hail is severe enough to cause your horse distress, dismount, turn his quarters to the wind, and place a jacket over his head to protect it, if he will allow you.

Thunderstorms

Thunder is always accompanied by lightning: if you can hear it, you are potentially within striking range. Long before that, your horse may become unsettled as he senses changes in air pressure.

The moment you hear the first rumble of thunder, head immediately for cover; if the noise scares your horse, use your voice to reassure him, and dismount if you are at risk of being thrown or losing control of him. Look for shelter in the form of a barn or similar substantial four-sided, fully enclosed building; picnic and rain shelters, rocky overhangs, car ports and open garages may keep you dry but are not safe shelters from lightning. Don't take refuge under an isolated tree, either, as lightning is most likely to strike the tallest object in the area; it can also travel some sixty feet along the ground after striking an object, so keep well clear of anything that is likely to attract a strike. Stay in your shelter until at least thirty minutes after you hear the last thunderclap.

If you are caught out in the open miles away from safe cover, you can reduce the chances of being struck by lightning by taking the following precautions.

● Keep away from water, telephone lines, power cables and metal objects such as wire fencing.
● If on high ground, move to a lower area, though stay clear of any riverbeds in case of flash flooding. If you are in a forest, head for a lower stand of trees.
● Dismount and tie your horse to a low bush, not a tree or fence.

Head for safety if a storm threatens. (Courtesy RAD Photographic)

- Crouch down with your feet touching together and your head low. Do not touch the ground with your hands.
- If you are in a group, spread out. If anyone is hit, be assured that an injured person will not retain an electrical charge so it is safe to touch them.

Hot Weather

Some horses cope better with hot weather than others, but nevertheless try to avoid exercising during the hottest parts of the day. *See also* page 92, Summer Horse Care.

Snow

If it starts to snow while you are out, it can quickly become very slippery underfoot, even with only a thin covering of snow on the ground. As well as affecting your vision, falling snowflakes can quickly settle on you and your horse, concealing any hi-vis clothing you are wearing and making you harder for motorists to see. Make your way home as quickly as you can safely do so. Remember that melting snow as well as heavy rain can cause flash floods.

Riding in Snow

Horses that work barefoot or in hoofboots won't have trouble with snow balling up in the feet, but shod horses can end up walking on frozen stilts and thereby run the risk of straining something as well as of stumbling and falling. Greasing the soles of the feet using vegetable oil or petroleum jelly only helps to a limited extent, and is not a solution you can rely on completely.

Snow also conceals the ground underfoot, making it impossible to avoid hazards such as potholes, icy patches, frozen ruts and discarded rubbish. Furthermore if you need to travel along, or cross other roads, there is an increased risk of motorists losing control of their vehicles.

While a specialist winter riding holiday in a place such as Sweden can be an amazing, safely managed experience, in most cases riding out in snow in the UK is just not worth the risk. Turn your horse out instead – many enjoy playing in it, and he'll be better able to cope with conditions underfoot without you on his back.

- Learn how to read the sky for signs of impending problems: the knowledge could make the difference between reaching shelter safely, or getting caught out in potentially hazardous conditions.

RIDING IN COLD WEATHER

During cold weather it helps if you at least start off warm, so try some brisk physical exercise before going out for a ride. Dress appropriately for the weather, too: if you get wet you'll feel the cold far more, so invest in some really good waterproof outer clothing. Choose a jacket with a collar you can turn up, and which has vents at the back and is long enough so you are not constantly sitting on it, or finding that rain is being channelled down on to the saddle. Full-length coats are expensive but can be a good investment if you have to ride out in the rain frequently, although take care when mounting and dismounting as they can sometimes interfere with your movement: the leg straps to keep the lower parts of the jacket from flapping around can get caught around the back of the saddle when dismounting, so for safety and to minimize damage to the coat, choose Velcro rather than buckle fasteners.

Waterproof overtrousers or chaps will keep you dry and can also increase warmth by reducing wind chill and adding an extra layer (see also page 27, What to Wear). Make sure the gap between the bottom of your jacket and the top of your boots is protected from becoming chilled; this will also help protect the upper thigh area from chilblains. Padded over-trousers or ski bottoms can also keep you pleasantly snug, though make sure you can mount and dismount in them easily. You can also buy an exercise sheet or a rain sheet specially designed for you to share with your horse, which will help to keep your upper legs dry and reduce chill – though some do need assistance from another person to fit.

Underneath, avoid tight-fitting garments, and wear layers of light clothing, as the air trapped between each layer will act as insulation. The innermost layer should be made of a fabric that will wick perspiration away from your skin.

- Ladies' tights can be an economical way of adding an extra layer beneath your jodhpurs in winter. That goes for men, too: no one need know your secret!

LOOK AFTER THE EXTREMITIES!

Buy thermal and water-resistant gloves to keep the hands warm and dry; grips on the palms and fingers will make it easier to keep hold of wet reins. Layering works as well for feet as for the rest of your body, but leave enough room to wiggle your toes. Replace leaky boots, as wet feet quickly become cold feet. You can also get hat covers that incorporate a cosy balaclava style face and neck warmer, although check it doesn't interfere with your peripheral vision.

MAKE USE OF ACCESSORIES

During cold weather, a seatsaver can be a wonderful accessory; and if you're going to be out in an isolated area, pack a space blanket for emergencies. Another useful cold weather accessory is a pocket handwarmer; disposable or rechargeable gel packs are easy to activate in any conditions.

● If you find yourself getting very chilled, try dismounting and walking briskly alongside your horse to warm up again.

WINTER HORSE CARE

Exercise

If your horse's exercise is limited by the weather, reduce his concentrate ration, substituting this with plenty of high fibre and low energy forage instead. Turn him out as much as possible as this will help to some extent in maintaining fitness, as well as reducing boredom and the likelihood of overfreshness due to over-confinement in the stable.

Clipping

Exercise will cause your horse to sweat even when the weather is very cold; a heavy winter coat increases this likelihood, and it will also take him longer to cool down and dry off. There can also be a risk of chilling, because a wet coat loses its insulating properties and conducts heat rapidly away from the body: a wet horse – whether from sweat or rain – loses body heat twenty times faster than a dry one.

Clipping a part or all of your horse's coat, depending on his workload, will allow him to work harder with less distress as well as making it easier to cool and dry him afterwards. Clipping is usually done once the winter coat has set – around October in the UK – and again as necessary until January. If you decide not to clip your horse, you can still hack him out, but you will need to go more slowly, and should allow extra time to cool him down and dry him off on your return.

Exercise and Rain Sheets

If your horse is clipped, an exercise sheet can help keep him warm in cold weather, especially on slower rides. On wet days a rain sheet (buy a lined one for use in cold weather) will keep your horse drier so it takes less time to dry him off when you get home. Choose breathable fabrics, preferably hi-vis, and make sure a fillet string is attached to prevent the sheet from being blown up over his quarters.

Dehydration

Dehydration can occur during the winter as well as the hot summer months; horses tend to drink less if the water is very cold, so top up water buckets with hot water to take the chill off. Clean water should also be constantly available to your horse in his field and stable: in freezing conditions check the surface has not frozen over, as this can be another cause of dehydration.

Leg Care

On returning from your ride, hooves should be picked out and washed off using a soft-bristled waterbrush to remove mud. Either allow the legs to dry naturally – this process can be speeded up by using bandages or travel leg wraps – and brush them off once dry, or wash them to remove mud. Use tepid rather than cold water, and don't scrub hard, as this can damage the skin surface, making it vulnerable to infection.

It is as well to keep feathering and heels clipped during the winter months, as this makes it easier to clean off mud and speeds up the drying process. It is also easier to spot any injuries, or the first signs of skin problems such as mud fever and cracked heels.

Caring for the Wet Horse

Although you should aim to bring your horse home cool, he may not be dry. If he is wet, either with sweat or rain, put a 'cooler' on him (unless you are lucky enough to have a washing and drying room): this is a special type of rug that wicks moisture away from the coat, helping

CARING FOR WET SADDLERY

Use a clean, damp cloth to wipe off sweat and dirt, then allow leather saddlery to dry naturally, away from any direct heat sources. Then you can apply a proprietary leather dressing, according to the manufacturer's instructions. If you have synthetic saddlery, follow the manufacturer's directions as to care.

it to dry quickly while keeping your horse warm. Leave him in his stable until he is dry enough to groom and rug up.

Your horse should be clean and dry before putting his usual turnout or stable rug on, otherwise chafing or skin infections may result. The only exception to this is if you own one of the new specialist turnout rugs with a lining that wicks away moisture to the breathable outer fabric, and which the manufacturer claims can safely be put on a wet horse. This does not apply to all 'breathable' turnout rugs, however – if you are not sure, check with the manufacturer as to the rug's suitability and uses.

● Remember to allow plenty of time to return home from a ride: darkness falls more quickly as well as earlier during the winter.

7 Activities

WARMING UP

Warming your horse up properly is as important when hacking as competing. It prepares the body gradually for the demands made on it and reduces the risk of injury – cold muscles and tendons don't work very efficiently and are more susceptible to damage. Failure to spend sufficient time warming up can also lead to your horse feeling uncomfortable and being unable to respond correctly.

How to Warm Up

Don't assume that because your horse has just come in from the field he's all warmed up and ready to go. Horses out at grass generally move fairly sedately as they graze from one patch to another, and although this gentle movement is preferable to being cooped up in a stable, it doesn't constitute a proper warm-up.

The length of time needed to warm up varies between individuals: pay attention to how your horse is moving, and let that, rather than your watch, dictate what you ask him to do. In colder weather allow more time for warming up, especially with older horses. If it is particularly cold or your horse is clipped, use an exercise blanket (see page 34, Saddlery). The after-effects of work done on previous days, and age and health issues such as arthritis, may also affect how long your warm-up takes.

Don't be tempted to hurry straight into trot: always start off at walk, asking your horse to move actively into the rein contact rather than slopping around on a long rein. Only introduce trot when you feel the stride becoming longer and freer, with more of a swing.

Pre-Riding Warm-Up Exercises

Before getting on your horse you can, if you wish, use a few exercises to help prepare your horse for work; they can also help you to relax. The following special 'TTouches' form part of the Tellington-Touch Equine Awareness Method (TTEAM) (see page 8), and can make a useful contribution towards warming and suppling up your horse. They take only a few minutes to do, are easily incorporated into your grooming and saddling up routine, and will help make your horse feel physically more comfortable and mentally more settled at the beginning of each session.

Jellyfish Jiggle

As well as helping to warm up your horse before riding, this TTouch helps to keep muscles from tightening after exercise:

- Place one hand lightly on your horse and the other on the muscled area of his neck. Using the fingers and palm of your hand, make soft, upward jiggling movements to the skin, creating an upward wave of movement.
- Cover all the muscled area of the neck like this, then the shoulder muscles, croup and

Jellyfish jiggle. (Sarah Fisher, courtesy **Horse & Rider** *magazine)*

hindquarters. Use both hands together, parallel to each other and with the fingers nearly touching when working on larger areas of muscle such as the quarters and croup.

Lick of the Cow's Tongue

This exercise raises the back, softens stiff, tight back muscles, enhances suppleness and coordination, and soothes sore, overworked muscles after a hard workout:

● Standing by the side of your horse next to the girth area, stroke gently with the back of your hand along his sides and belly. If he is happy for you to do this, lightly place one hand flat on his body. Place your other hand under the belly just past the midline, keeping the fingers slightly apart, gently curved and pointing away from your own body.

● Draw your hand up the belly towards you in a long, sweeping stroke. As it moves up your horse's side, rotate it so the fingers point upwards, and continue the upward sweep, up to and just over the spine.

● Repeat, placing your hand one hand's width across from the first one until you have covered the whole of the belly area – if your horse is ticklish around the flanks, just work on those areas where he is comfortable.

THIS PAGE & OPPOSITE TOP: *Lick of the cow's tongue. (Sarah Fisher, courtesy* Horse & Rider *magazine)*

Leg Circles

Doing these circles on all four legs enhances the flexibility of the limbs and shoulder and neck muscles, encourages breathing, improves balance and helps release tension in the horse's back. If you repeat them after putting the saddle on, it is also a more comfortable way of preventing wrinkles gathering in front of the girth than pulling the legs forwards.

- Stand next to your horse, facing towards the quarters. Stroke down the back of the foreleg closest to you with one hand, and ask him to pick up his foot by squeezing the back of the leg just above the fetlock between finger and thumb.
- Support the fetlock joint with the hand closest to your horse, and cradle the hoof

with the other. Keep your thumb over the shoe and the fingers cupping the front of the hoof; point the toe towards the ground to avoid flexing the fetlock joint. Keep your hips and knee joints flexed, and rest your outside elbow on your outside knee or thigh to protect your back.

- Gently circle the hoof the same number of times in both directions, just above the spot on the ground where it was resting. Allow the movement to be created by circling your body, rather than just your hands – this makes it a smoother movement.
- Circle the hoof at gradually decreasing distances from the ground until the toe is finally resting on it. Do not lift the hoof higher or make the circles bigger than your horse is comfortable with, and do not draw the leg out to one side.

Leg circles. (Sarah Fisher, courtesy **Horse & Rider** *magazine)*

- Repeat with the other foreleg, and then with each of the hind legs. When lifting a back foot, support the cannon bone rather than the fetlock joint with your inside hand.

Rainbow TTouch

This TTouch promotes circulation in the lower legs, and energizes and heightens your horse's awareness of his lower limbs.

- Stand slightly to the side of your horse, facing towards his quarters. Starting at the top, place one hand on the inside of the front leg closest to you, the other opposite it on the outside of the leg.
- Move both hands at the same time, sliding them in an arc-like movement in opposite directions as well as on opposite sides of the leg. As the hand on the outside of the leg moves forwards from the front to the back of the leg, the one on the inside simultaneously moves from the back towards the front, and vice versa on the next arc.
- Work down the entire length of the leg in a continuous series of arcs, then repeat with the other front leg. Try it with the hind legs too, but only if your horse is happy with the front leg work, and can be trusted not to kick. Stand to the side of your horse, facing towards his head as you work on each hind leg.

Rainbow TTouch.

beneficial, helping him to arrive home cool and mentally relaxed.

WARMING DOWN

Warming down is as important as warming up properly; it stretches tired muscles, reduces the risk of muscular stiffness, and helps in the elimination of the waste products of exertion. Try to walk at least the last mile of your ride so you arrive home cool and with your horse in a relaxed frame of mind. If he is still hot and sweating, walk him until he is cool, and if the weather is cold, use a cooler (a type of breathable rug) to help wick moisture away from his skin, which will keep him from

Hacking to Shows or Lessons

Hacking to a lesson or show can be a good way of loosening up your horse, forming part of his warm-up. Make sure you leave sufficient time to get there without hurrying. Around thirty minutes is probably about as long a ride as you want to consider, bearing in mind that your horse will then be working hard, after which he has to walk home again. Provided it's not an excessive distance, the walk home can also be becoming chilled. (*See also* page 101, and page 92, Summer Horse Care.)

Some of the TTouches used as part of a warm-up (*see* page 102, Warming Up) can be used after you have finished your ride; take the saddle off but leave the saddlecloth on and do Lick of the Cow's Tongue, and Jellyfish Jiggles. Most horses enjoy TTouches, so they are also a nice way of thanking him as well as helping him recover after work.

Post-Ride Checks

Always spend a few minutes carefully checking your horse over after a ride:

- As you remove the bridle look for signs of bruising or cuts on the tongue, gums and corners of the lips, and run your hands over the whole of the rest of his body and down each leg in turn: if you are wearing gloves, remove them so you can easily detect any heat, swellings or signs of soreness.
- Look for hair that has been rubbed the wrong way by friction from saddlery: checking the marks on the underside of the saddlecloth can tell you a lot about the even (or otherwise) distribution of pressure from the rider and saddle.
- If the legs and feet are muddy, wash them off with tepid water to make it easier to examine them properly (*see* page 101): lift up each foot in turn and pick them out. Overreach wounds – where the heel of a front foot has been injured by the toe of a back foot – can be easy to miss as they often involve a flap of skin which can conceal the wound, so examine this area carefully.
- Check that the horse's breathing is normal, and if you've been out longer or asked more of your horse than usual, check him over again later on to ensure he is comfortable.

Minor cuts are usually easily dealt with by gentle hosing or cleaning with a diluted antiseptic or saline solution (add a teaspoon of salt to each pint/500ml boiled water). Do not probe around in the wound as you may push dirt in deeper. Grazes and puncture wounds may need poulticing to help draw out any dirt. Trimming the hair away from the edges of the wound will help you assess it more easily. Call the vet in the following circumstances:

- If the wound looks as though it may need stitching.
- If it looks as if there is a foreign body inside.
- If it involves a joint.
- If the horse is very lame.
- If his anti-tetanus vaccinations are not up to date.

RIDING ALONE

Although there are many reasons why it is preferable to hack out with another rider, this may not always be possible – and sometimes a quiet chill-out for just you and your horse is precisely what you need.

When riding out by yourself, always take a mobile phone, and tell someone where you are going and how long you expect to be. Make sure that the person you tell is someone who will still be at the yard and will notice if you don't come back, not someone who will have gone home and forgotten all about you. Agree a time for them to alert searchers to look for you if you haven't returned.

Keep to the route you've decided on so that search parties will know where to look for you; if you change your mind or have to take a detour, use your mobile phone to ring and tell the person of your change of plan. And don't forget to let them know when you do get back!

- If no one is around, a whiteboard near your horse's stable with a 'Where I've gone' section is a good idea.

Riding is a social occasion for many riders, and it can be nice to have company and someone to chat to. (Courtesy RAD Photographic)

Passing Other Riders

If you come across another rider and need to overtake, make sure the other person is aware of your presence and ask if it's all right to pass before doing so. Pass at a steady trot, giving the other horse a wide berth.

RIDING IN COMPANY

Going out with another rider means that if anything happens help is at hand, and if further assistance is needed it will be promptly summoned. A more experienced, steady and reliable horse can also be a settling influence on a younger, inexperienced horse, and can give a calm lead when tackling new hazards for the first time.

Riding in Single File

Always ride in single file where roads are narrow, when passing a parked car, when approaching a tight bend, or wherever visibility is otherwise poor, such as the approach to a hump-backed bridge. The person at the front should give those following plenty of warning of any change of gait or change in terrain, or of any hazards ahead. If there are more than eight riders in the party, it is advisable to ride in smaller groups with a gap of at least twenty-five metres between you to make it easier and safer for vehicles to pass.

● When in single file keep a horse's length apart – so you can just see the hocks of the horse in front when looking through your own horse's ears – so you aren't close enough to provoke, or be on the receiving end of a kick.

Crossing a Road

When crossing a road, do so as a group rather than in ones and twos. If you are a large party, two riders should station themselves in the middle of the road, one on each side of the group and ask traffic to stop by using the appropriate hand signals (*see* page 72, Hand Signals).

Riding Abreast

Riding abreast with someone makes it easier to chat, and because you take up more of the carriageway, it can encourage motorists to slow down before overtaking – but only do so on roads that are wide enough to permit this safely. On narrow roads or where there are bends, undulations or other hazards affecting visibility, riders should resume single file. Don't get so absorbed in chatting that you lose track of what's going on around you.

When riding double on roads, less experienced horses should be placed on the inside, furthest away from passing traffic. Don't get so close to each other that your stirrups lock together or your horses feel crowded, when they might be more inclined to nip at each other or kick. If one begins to pull faces, check your distance and turn its head in the opposite direction so it can't intimidate the other horse, or revert to riding in single file.

Walkie-talkies

It may be worth considering the advantages of investing in a two-way walkie-talkie system, primarily as a good way of communicating with other riders in your group if you become separated. For ride escorts they can be useful when taking out larger groups or riding in areas such as woodland, where riders at the rear may not always be visible. Look for a tough, hands-free unit with a single earpiece, and check as to whether a licence is required.

LEADING A HORSE

Leading a Horse from Another Horse

Riding one horse and leading another can be a helpful way of exercising two horses when time is at a premium, or of taking nervous riders out; however, never attempt it with horses likely to be fractious with each other. Both horses should wear brushing boots on all four legs: put overreach or coronet boots on the rear feet of the ridden horse and on the front feet of the lead horse to protect them both from tread injuries. Practise riding and leading at home in a safe enclosed area before attempting it on roads, making sure you can stop, start, turn and give hand signals. The led horse should wear a

NOTES FOR RIDE ESCORTS

- A single ride escort should be sufficient to accompany a group of four to six competent riders; larger numbers than this, or a group of less experienced riders, will require at least two or more escorts.
- When taking out large groups, the rear escort could be equipped with a whistle to signal to the ride leader at the front in the event of needing to stop, or of a problem: the horses must, however, be used to it, and not likely to be spooked.
- Explain to riders before setting out how to gauge the correct distance from the horse in front.
- Ride escorts should be sufficiently familiar with the horses so that they know where best to place them within the ride. Any horse that is inclined to kick should be positioned at the rear.
- The escort leading the ride should remain positioned at the front so they can control what is going on behind. Where the riders are sufficiently experienced, the ride leader can drop back to ride abreast of the second file, but shouldn't allow any of the ride to draw ahead of them in case a problem is encountered.
- A rear escort should remain at the back of the ride when on roads, but otherwise can be more flexible in position, moving to wherever

assistance may be appropriate. This should not be an excuse for cantering back and forth: move at a steady gait so as not to overexcite or overtire the escort horse, or to excite those of the rest of the ride.
- The lead escort should keep an eye on what is going on behind them as well as in front, so they are immediately aware of any riders having difficulties. Don't allow the ride to become too spread out – if anyone is getting left behind, slow down or wait for them. The speed the lead escort rides at should always be geared to the least capable rider.
- Both front and rear ride escorts should be ready to encourage and offer advice where necessary, correcting positions, helping with any difficulties, and ensuring correct distances are maintained. Be authoritative but not rude. If you ask a rider to do something, explain why, but insist your instructions are followed.
- The least experienced riders should be given the quietest horses, and positioned to the centre of the group.
- During the ride, escorts should keep a close watch to front and rear and give guidance to any traffic coming from both directions.
- Always double check that everyone has heard your instructions, especially when planning to increase speed or when negotiating hazards.

snaffle bridle, and either the reins or a leadrope used to lead it.

If you have help, the led horse can be handed to you once you are mounted. If you are on your own, tack up both horses and tie them up. Check your own saddlery, tighten the girth, and pull down both stirrups. Untie the led horse and stand him at right angles to the ridden horse, with his head positioned just in front of the

nearside shoulder so you have space to mount.

Ride with the flow of traffic, keeping the led horse to your left so you are between him and the traffic. Hold the reins of your horse in your right hand and the reins or leadrope of the led horse in your left hand, with the remaining length in your right.

Encourage the led horse to stay level with your left knee: if he gets too far forward or lags

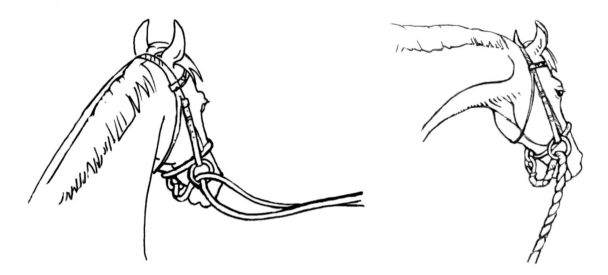

If leading with the reins, take them over the horse's head and thread the near-side rein through the off-side bit ring. If using a leadrope, pass it through the off-side bit ring, beneath the jaw and clip it to the near-side bit ring.

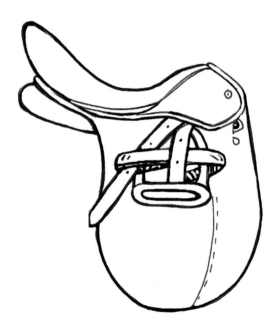

Secure your stirrups when leading your horse so they won't flap around or become caught on anything.

behind you will have less control, and could be pulled off as well as increasing the risk of nipping, barging and of leg injuries.

When dismounting, halt both horses, then ask the one you are riding to do a quarter turn on the forehand (*see* page 116, Schooling) so they are facing at right angles to each other (as when mounting) and you have room to get off.

Leading a Horse While on Foot

If you need to dismount and lead your horse, run up and secure both stirrups so they can't slide down, and unless planning to remount within a few minutes, loosen the girth slightly. Even if he is wearing a headcollar under the bridle, either attach your leadrope to the bit, or take the reins over his head (*see* illustration) for maximum control. If leading with the bridle reins, remove the running martingale from them if one is used.

When on roads, lead your horse with the flow of traffic, positioning yourself on his off (right-hand) side so you are between him and passing vehicles. This means that overtaking vehicles will pass at a greater distance from him, and makes it easier for you to prevent his quarters from swinging into passing traffic. Leading him from this side may be strange to him, so practise at home to ensure he will lead freely from either side.

Wear hi-vis clothing, and in conditions of poor visibility carry a light showing white to the front and red to the rear in your right hand to increase your visibility to motorists.

Taking a Rider on a Leadrein

The rider should always be allowed to keep the bridle reins: use a leadrein attached to the bit either by threading it through the bit rings (see illustration) or using bit couplings. Otherwise the procedure for leading is as described above.

● To ensure you have as much control as possible, never lead more than one horse at a time.

NOTES FOR RIDE ESCORTS

● When leading a rider from horseback, keep the horse up alongside so it is easy to observe the rider's position, and so you can speak without having to shout. For comfort and safety, pick an escort horse that can work comfortably at a similar speed to the led horse.
● All ride escorts should carry a leadrein and be capable of taking a horse or pony on the lead rein if necessary.

REPORTING INCIDENTS

The following numbers work across the United Kingdom and allow you to quickly report unusual activity or incidents:

● Rural crime: call Crimestoppers anonymously on 0800 555 111 or 999 in an emergency
● Pollution, fly tipping, dead fish: call the Environment Agency on 0800 80 70 60
● Anti-terrorist hotline: 0800 789 321
● Forest and heathland fires: call 999

ENJOYING THE SCENERY

One of the best places to enjoy a great view is from on horseback – you'll notice things you'd miss when in a car or even on a pushbike, and have the advantage of height and the ability to cover more ground than on foot. Wildlife is less likely to be scared off, you can hear and enjoy birdsong, follow an otter along the riverbank as he fishes his beat, and enjoy all the beauties of the changing seasons.

When hacking out you are also in a good position to protect the countryside and generate some positive publicity for horse riders at the same time. Keeping your eyes open can prevent or reduce theft from farms, fly tipping, fires, river pollution and cruelty to

NOTES FOR RIDE ESCORTS

Making the effort to find out about the wildlife and other features of interest in the area you are passing through, and then sharing your knowledge with your clients, can add interest to the ride for them.

wildlife. Wherever you live, find out local emergency numbers and programme them into your mobile phone. If you do see something suspicious, don't get involved: simply report the matter promptly with as much information as you can (especially any vehicle registration details) and follow the advice you are given.

CANTERING AND GALLOPING

Cantering while out hacking can be an exhilarating experience, and even more so when the horse increases his speed and gallops. It's very different from cantering in the school, however, and you should take a few precautions.

First of all, your horse needs to be fit enough: if he's fat and unfit it can damage his limbs and respiratory system; he should also have plenty of time to warm up in walk and trot. Furthermore you need to be competent enough to cope: learn how to canter in a safely enclosed area before you attempt it out hacking. Some horses may get a little headstrong when moving at speed, so if it's your first time cantering or galloping out on a ride, or if your horse is new to you, select a piece of ground which slopes uphill, as this will make it easier for you to keep control and to slow down.

Make sure the ground is suitable: never canter along roadside verges in case your horse suddenly spooks out into the path of passing vehicles. Ride the line of your intended canter at walk first to check for hazards and to assess the

Cantering while out on a ride can be fun but should also be done selectively and with care.
(Courtesy RAD Photographic)

NOTES FOR RIDE ESCORTS

Good discipline and ride control are essential when cantering on a hack:

- Remember that horses are herd animals and prefer to remain as a group. It is therefore inadvisable to split the ride in two so those who want to canter can, while the rest remain in walk or trot, as it offers too many opportunities for riders to lose control.
- Always conduct rides at gaits the weakest rider can cope with: where you have a group of mixed abilities this may mean not cantering. Proficient riders may find this frustrating, so try to place them on rides appropriate to their level of competence.
- Try to choose areas where it is hard for anyone to overtake you if they do lose control, so you can keep them behind you.

- Be sure to brief riders before you canter, explaining that they are not to race or overtake, and must maintain their distance between each other.
- Riders at the rear may have the idea of holding their horses back at the beginning of the canter so they can gallop on to catch up: this notion should be nipped in the bud, and explain that if this does happen, there will be no more cantering on the ride.
- Give plenty of warning that you are going to canter, and slow down gradually, so riders don't crash into the quarters of the horse in front. Moving from walk into trot before taking canter, and into trot before slowing to walk will also be less unseating for riders, and less strain on the horses' legs.

state of the going. Ideally the surface should be fairly even and with a certain amount of give in it – the hooves should sink in for about an inch. If it is softer and deeper than this, the risk of strains increases, and if it is harder it will jar his legs and feet, potentially leading to concussion-related injuries (*see* page 65, Hard Ground).

Be on your guard if riding next to a hedge or fencing as it may harbour wildlife: any unexpected noise or movement may make your horse shy, and it's much harder to stay in the saddle if this happens while moving at speed. Beaches can be great places to canter, but you may need to choose your time carefully (*see* page 122, Beach Rides).

Begin slowing down in plenty of time so you don't run out of space – it may take longer than when you are cantering in the school or field at home.

If cantering or galloping in company, don't

race each other, as it can get out of hand. Allow more excitable horses to go in front, and be ready to slow down or stop if you see they are getting strong or the rider is struggling to keep control. Avoid always cantering or galloping in the same places, as this can lead to anticipation and misbehaviour (*see also* page 135, Bolting).

JUMPING

Popping over the occasional natural obstacle you come across can be fun, but if you've never jumped before or have very limited experience of it, take a few lessons and practise in the safety of an enclosed area before trying it out on a ride.

Never jump anything without first checking both the take-off and landing sides, even if it's

If you enjoy jumping, many sponsored rides include optional natural fences that can be jumped along the route, and you can also combine hacking and jumping at many toll rides around the country. (Courtesy RAD Photographic)

an obstacle you have jumped before – don't assume it will still be safe. Don't jump anything out hacking that you wouldn't attempt at home, or construct obstacles across paths, or jump anything potentially unsafe: look out for wire on or near it, or fallen tree trunks with broken or twiggy branches sticking up. Be prepared for a bigger jump when out on a hack than your horse might produce at home: take a handful of mane or use the neckstrap to make sure you don't get left behind or become unbalanced.

SCHOOLING

Schooling is as important for hacking horses as those which compete – it helps make your horse a more supple, manoeuvrable, obedient and comfortable ride, it will increase his surefootedness and make him less prone to injury, and it plays a part in forming a harmonious partnership based on trust and good communication.

Although it is easiest to introduce new exercises in an area where there aren't too many distractions, you can also school while out hacking. It can even have advantages as it tends to be less repetitive, encourages free forward movement, teaches your horse to work in many different environments and situations (invaluable if you compete), and is likely to include many more rest breaks in between each mini work session than you might normally include when schooling at home. These breaks are important as they give your horse the opportunity to stretch, relax, and mentally and physically process what he's just done.

There are several schooling movements that you might try in the course of a hack:

Transitions: Ride both progressive and non-progressive transitions – and don't forget to include some halts as well. Try riding for a set number of steps or strides within each gait; this is a good way to increase your own feel and timing of the aids, as well as improving accuracy, balance and impulsion.

Gait variants: As well as riding transitions to and from a gait, ride transitions within them, and ask for both shortened and lengthened strides.

Serpentine loops: A serpentine is a simple but excellent suppling exercise that will help reduce one-sidedness (*see* page 119). The loops can be shallow or deeper depending on the width of track you are on, but try to make them a similar length.

Flexion: Practise asking for left flexion and right flexion – and also keeping your horse's head and neck absolutely straight while riding him forwards in a straight line. This can be helpful preparation for lateral work, and encourages you to use your legs to maintain straightness rather than your hands. It is also a useful exercise to help make you aware of, and to remedy, one-sided tendencies (*see* page 119).

Leg yield: Hacking can be a great time to practise this exercise as you will be less inclined to over-exaggerate the sideways movement and to maintain forward impulsion. Ride zigzag lines in leg yield from left to right and right to left, and practise left and right leg yield at an angle to the track.

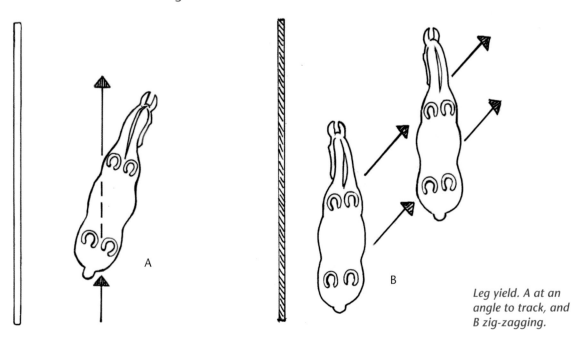

Leg yield. A at an angle to track, and B zig-zagging.

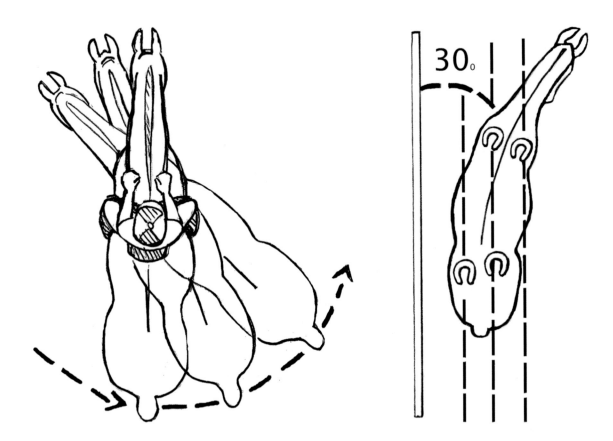

TOP LEFT: *Turn on the forehand.*

TOP RIGHT: *Shoulder-in.*

Turn about the forehand and turn on the forehand: When asking for a turn on the forehand you don't need to do a full or half turn – try asking for just one or two steps and then straightening your horse and riding forwards again. This teaches precision and control, as well as increasing suppleness through your horse's hips, and means you don't need a great deal of space to the side, nor will you end up facing in the opposite direction to which you want to go. It is a useful exercise to improve manoeuvrability in tight spaces, and together with leg yield, will make it easier to open and shut gates while mounted.

Shoulder-in: This is an important exercise for hacking horses because as well as increasing freedom of movement through the shoulders and promoting impulsion through engagement of the quarters and lightening of the forehand, it can be invaluable when passing spooky objects (*see* page 159, Shying and Spooking).

SAFETY

Be very careful when doing schooling exercises while out hacking: never put yourself or others at risk. Be observant and use common sense to decide which exercises are safe in which environments, and when it's best to wait for a more suitable spot to try them.

One-Sidedness

Horses that hack out a lot often become very one-sided, largely due to the rider having to check frequently over their right shoulder for traffic, and having to maintain a degree of right flexion to help control the quarters and any potential spooking (*see* page 159, Shying and Spooking). This tends to produce a crooked rider, too, inclined to sit to the left and collapse through the right side of the waist. Rider crookedness directly affects the horse's straightness, balance, athleticism and sure-footedness, and can be a cause of back injury for both horse and rider. This is something that is difficult to check by yourself, so take whatever assistance you can get: regular lessons are a big help, and when riding out with a friend, take it in turns to check on and correct each other.

The less one-sided your horse is, the more comfortable to ride and easy to manoeuvre he will be, so anything you can do to minimize this tendency is worth doing. As well as schooling exercises, change diagonals from time to time when in trot. Your horse may feel more comfortable on one trotting diagonal than the other, and some can be very good at throwing you to the more comfortable one without you noticing, so check occasionally in case this has happened. Note also any difference in stride length and how comfortable *you* feel when you change to a different diagonal, as it can be an indication of how one-sided your horse is.

Trotting diagonals: You are on the left diagonal when the sitting phase of your rising trot coincides with the moment that the horse's left fore and right hind touch the ground – glance downwards and you will see the left shoulder moving back towards you. You are on the right diagonal when the right fore and left hind touch the ground (as the right shoulder moves back towards you). It doesn't matter which diagonal you are on when out hacking as long as you change it periodically, trying to

NOTE FOR RIDE ESCORTS

There are usually plenty of opportunities where you can make the ride an educational as well as a pleasurable experience – most riders enjoy being able to put skills learned in the school to practical use.

spend an equal amount of time on each. Change the diagonal by sitting for an extra beat of the trot; if you have any difficulty doing this, ask your riding teacher for help.

DAY RIDES

Once you've discovered all the possibilities on your immediate doorstep, you may decide to explore further afield by going on longer rides that take you further from home: this can add a whole new dimension to your hacking, when you never quite know exactly what lies round the next corner. This will need some advance planning, as your horse needs to be fit enough to cope with the extra distance as well as the type of terrain if it changes dramatically. You could even go further still if you make it a weekend outing rather than just a day out, in which case you will also need to arrange overnight accommodation (*see* page 126, Taking your Horse on Holiday).

Travelling Further Afield

Taking your horse off in a horsebox or trailer will enable you to explore new rides even further away. If you do this, it is important to take into account the amount of time your horse spends travelling, because in coping with the constant movement he expends more energy than

If travelling, know where you are going to park. If there are height restriction barriers on car park entrances, arrange in advance for them to be opened. Different parking charges may apply for trailers and boxes than for cars.

walking: each hour of journey time should be considered as the equivalent of an hour's exercise.

Provide a well soaked haynet that he can pick at during the journey to help minimize risk of dehydration, and make sure you take water with you so you can offer your horse a drink. Even if there is a water supply at your destination, some horses can be reluctant to drink water that tastes different to their usual supply. Adding apple juice can help disguise the taste and flavour, but unless a horse is already accustomed to this, it may make some horses even more suspicious.

If your horse is a bad loader or poor traveller, spend time trying to improve this before taking your horse out, otherwise mental and physical stress may mean he reaches his destination already fatigued; this will also increase the likelihood of him becoming dehydrated.

Plan Ahead

● Research your route, checking on access to and from bridleways and any sections of road which may be busy. Look for places to stop along the way, where you can have a bite to eat and can water your horse; enquire in advance whether you will be welcome, as not all pub landlords will appreciate a horse trampling over the beer garden.

- Standard roadside recovery policies may not include handling horses if you break down. Arrange specialist cover if necessary.
- Before setting off, walk round your vehicle to check that all the latches are secure, and double check that you have everything you need.
- At your destination, secure both car and trailer before setting off, and don't leave anything lying around in your eagerness to get going, as it may not be there when you get back!
- Leave a card with your contact details easily visible inside a vehicle window. Include your mobile telephone number, and that of a responsible person back at home, in case there's a problem with your vehicle or where you've parked it. Only give phone numbers: don't show your address or an intended return time, as this can encourage theft.
- On your return, check your vehicle – in particular the hitch area of trailers – in case somebody has interfered with it while you have been away.
- Carry a shovel and an old feed sack so you can tidy up your horse's droppings before you leave.
- Don't forget you should take your horse's passport with you even if you are only going out for a couple of hours in the trailer or horsebox; if you are riding out from home it should be available at three hours' notice.

Taking a Break

If you want to tie up your horse during a rest break, choose a quiet area. If people show an interest in him, be polite, because at that moment in time you are an ambassador for the whole equine community. Explain why they shouldn't feed horses they don't know, and demonstrate how to approach them safely.

Always tie up using a leadrope attached to a headcollar, and never use the bridle reins – if the horse pulls back he could break the bridle and injure his mouth and neck. If you leave the bridle on over the top of his headcollar, twist the reins around each other under his neck and then thread the throatlash through them to keep them out of the way.

Use a quick release knot so you can free him quickly in an emergency, and tie him to a piece of breakable string in case you are unable to reach him in time. You can buy special breakaway ties, or carry pre-cut lengths of string in your pocket for this purpose. The string or breakaway section should be attached to something fixed, which won't be moved or dislodged. Tie your horse up short enough that although comfortable, he can't get his head caught under the rope or a leg over it; the tie point needs to be at head level to prevent the latter from happening.

Always keep a close eye on your horse while he is tied up, as some may play with the rope and accidentally untie themselves. If your horse is liable to become spooked or has a habit of

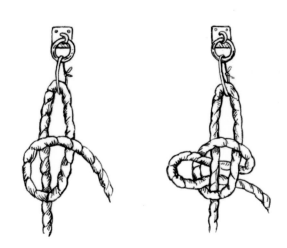

Quick release knot.

hanging back or breaking free when tied, then hold him instead.

If you remove the saddle, place it out of reach of your horse so it is not accidentally damaged: if you have to place it on the ground, rest it on the pommel.

On longer rides horses as well as riders may need to stop for a toilet break. Although they can defecate while on the move, they need to stop to urinate, and in this case will slow down or stop completely and stretch the hind legs out behind them, straddling them wide apart. If you are still mounted when this happens, take a handful of mane to support yourself and stand up in the stirrups; wait until he has finished and brought his back legs beneath him again before you settle back gently into the saddle. Some horses won't urinate while their rider is in the saddle, in which case you will need to get off when your horse shows signs of needing to spend a penny – stand well forward, by his head, so you don't get splashed.

Traditionally horse riders have rarely bothered to move their horse's droppings, irrespective of where this may occur. However, it is increasingly seen as courteous to get off and kick any droppings to the side of routes where it is likely to cause a nuisance to other people, such as on surfaced routes shared with families with prams, cyclists and people using wheelchairs.

BEACH RIDES

Beach rides can be great fun, although not without hazard. Some beaches are busier than others, but expect to meet up with at least a few alarming elements – in addition to pedestrians and loose dogs there may be kite fliers, paragliders, sand yachts, swimmers, anglers and sometimes even cars. Many beaches also contain partially covered relics of sea defences from the two world wars, such as cables, collapsed gun emplacements and tank traps, while strong storm tides can expose new hazards overnight. Lines of seaweed left at the

---

NOTES FOR RIDE ESCORTS

- Half, full day, pub or picnic rides usually prove very popular, but need good planning: if it's a new route, ride along it to check its suitability, and note any problem areas.
- If stopping at a pub for lunch, take bookings for food in advance and phone them through beforehand so all meals arrive at the same time. Arrange for sufficient helpers to meet you there and at other planned rest stops along the way to help with watering, tying up or holding horses, and with re-mounting clients when it is time to move on again. These helpers can also check the area to ensure no rubbish is left behind.
- If saddles are removed during the break, make sure that each one goes back on the horse it belongs to, and that girths are tightened before moving off.
- Clients may be not be used to spending more than an hour in the saddle, so encourage them to try a few stretching exercises during breaks, and if necessary be prepared to slow the pace. Be ready to assist when dismounting, as this is often a moment when tired muscles give out.
- If stopping at a pub, not all adults may be responsible about the amount of alcohol they consume. Keep a discreet eye on your clients' behaviour, and do not allow them to continue the ride if you feel their judgement is impaired; be diplomatic, but firm.

If you want to paddle your horse at the edge of the water, stay in walk as you don't know exactly what's beneath the surface. As well as rubbish and unlevel going, there can be surprises you hadn't anticipated – such as flatfish, which are often difficult to see and may brush against your horse's legs or cause an unexpected splash in the water. (Courtesy RAD Photographic)

high tide mark can conceal objects such as ropes and other litter from commercial fishing.

Be careful when passing rocky outcrops and boulders; the best thing to do is give them a wide berth, as some horses may be wary of the rocks themselves, and if a sunbather appears unexpectedly from behind one it may spook him.

In bays where access may depend on low water levels, make sure you know the tide times so you don't get cut off: details of these can be found in local newspapers or by checking on the internet. When the tide is out, a wide expanse of beach can look inviting to gallop on, but beware of boggy patches and soft sand. There is often no outwardly discernible difference between firm sand and quicksand, but the going can change within a stride, and the first you will know about it is when your horse puts one or more feet into a patch. If he is cantering or galloping at the time, he could easily break a leg.

Therefore walk the line you intend to canter or gallop first to check the going, looking out for nasties such as sharp stones and rubbish left by others or washed in by the sea. When riding on shingle, keep to walk as it can be hard work, and the unpredictable movement underfoot can lead to strains.

● The salty environment can be damaging to leather saddlery, so clean it thoroughly after your ride.

Getting your Feet Wet

Even a horse that is usually confident about going through water may be less certain when faced with the sea for the first time, as it will be bigger and noisier than he's used to, and there will be more movement from wavelets lapping around his legs. The company of another horse that is accustomed to it can help reassure him (*see also* page 69, Water).

If you want to swim with your horse, be responsible about it, from the point of view of safety, and also to ensure it is as much fun for your horse as for you. You'll need to find a beach with a gentle incline, rather than a sudden sharp drop; local riders or nearby riding schools that offer beach rides should be able to advise about the best places and times to go.

Choose a warm day, and if the sea is anything other than calm, postpone going in until another time. Once you have ventured into the water, ride up and down in the shallows parallel to the beach, gradually moving into deeper water as your horse gains in confidence. This may take several sessions to achieve, so be patient, building up gradually to going in belly deep and then higher until your horse is finally floating. The first time your horse finds he can't touch the bottom he may panic a little: speak reassuringly to him and steer him back towards the shore again.

When swimming, his legs will move in a powerful and exaggerated trotting or pacing gait, so stay on his back or floating just above it so you keep well clear of them and don't get kicked.

Swimming is very hard work for a horse, so don't overdo things: ten minutes is estimated to be the equivalent of an hour's intense schooling, so five minutes is more than enough for the first time.

Swimming Gear

For water work it is best to use a nylon web bridle as this won't be damaged by contact with the water; also wet horses are very slippery, so fit a neckstrap which you can hold for balance. Ride bareback – even if you have a synthetic saddle it will still get waterlogged, weighing your horse down and taking ages to dry out. Put synthetic brushing boots on, as there is an increased risk of your horse striking

into himself while swimming. Either remove your own shoes, or wear light trainers that won't get too waterlogged – and be sure to wear your hard hat.

Estuaries

Estuaries – areas where rivers meet the sea – can look as inviting to ride on as beaches, but they can be unpredictable so should be treated with caution. The terrain can vary from sand to shingle, rocks to mudflats and salt marshes; incoming tides can be fast, cutting off escape routes, and many have areas of quicksand. Wading birds often visit to feed at low tide, and although you should try to avoid disturbing them, if they take off as a flock they might startle your horse.

Estuaries often provide important but fragile habitats for wildlife: many are Sites of Special Scientific Interest (SSSIs), and access may be restricted at certain times, or prohibited: where it is permitted, stay on designated paths and tracks.

RIPTIDES

Be aware of the presence of riptides or dangerous currents that might cause you to get into difficulties: always seek and heed local advice. Riptides can happen in all sorts of weather and on all sorts of beaches: some are brief occurrences while others may be a feature of the area. A riptide is a narrow, very powerful water current which runs at a right angle from the shore out into the ocean. They can move fast, and trying to swim head on against one wastes valuable energy: instead, guide your horse so he swims parallel to the shore until free of the current, when you can head back towards the beach.

RIDING HOLIDAYS

Taking a riding holiday gives you the chance to spend more time in the saddle than you might usually, and options are available for all tastes. You can take a break in this country, or abroad if you fancy a more exotic location, or go on safari, camp out, or relax at the end of the day in luxury accommodation. Some holidays include instruction, the chance to learn new skills such as herding cattle, or may be purely trekking; you can go for a long weekend, a midweek break, a week, or longer – the choices are all yours. Other points to consider include the following:

What other activities are available? If you are going with family members who don't ride and are not interested in taking it up, select a holiday with additional activities and attractions to keep them happy while you are out riding.

What's included? Check what's included in the deal, because although food, drink, sightseeing trips and transfers to and from airports are often included, this isn't always the case and your holiday could end up costing more than you anticipated.

How much riding will you be doing? Ask how much riding you'll be getting, over what sort of terrain, and at what sort of speeds. If all you are used to is a sedate plod for an hour each week, more energetic and challenging rides might come as a considerable shock to your system. More seriously, it could also lead to injury or loss of confidence, so pick a holiday that is appropriate to your ability and fitness level.

How many people are in each group, and are they graded in any way? Some people like to be part of a large group, others prefer a smaller, more intimate one with more personal attention. Groups may be adults only, or they may include children – enquire about this if it is likely to affect your enjoyment of your holiday.

Be honest about your abilities to ensure that you are booking the right sort of holiday. Sometimes groups are made up of mixed abilities so will travel at a slow pace which you may find frustrating if you are more advanced: equally, if you are inexperienced or nervous you don't want to discover too late that you have been placed with a hugely confident party of riders you can't keep up with.

● Personal recommendation can be valuable, so pick the brains of friends and those on equine forums: look also for ABRS and/or BHS accreditation.

Be Prepared

The riding centre should be able to advise as to what to bring with you: if planning on a holiday abroad, check the list carefully as it may include extras you might not have thought of and which will help keep you comfortable and safe. Although it probably won't be suggested, you might also like to pack a seat saver for a little extra comfort!

Brochures and adverts often show riders cantering along wearing very little and bareheaded. Don't follow their example, but make sure you wear appropriate footwear, and a hard hat – take your own as it will be a correct fit (*see also* page 25, What to Wear).

Even if you are only planning on mooching along, accidents can as easily happen on holiday as at home, so make sure you have adequate insurance cover. Horse riding is considered a high risk activity by most companies, so don't assume that you are covered by basic holiday insurance or any other policies you may hold: read through them carefully to check, and make sure that emergency medical repatriation is also included.

● If you are not used to doing much riding, try to get a little fitter before you go (*see* page 16, Rider Fitness) so that your break isn't spoiled by excessive fatigue and aches and pains

TAKING YOUR HORSE ON HOLIDAY

Going on holiday doesn't mean having to leave your horse behind – you can always take him with you, either to a riding school or holiday centre, or plan your own tailor-made trail-riding break. Whichever option you decide on, make sure your horse will be fit enough, check that his worming programme and vaccinations are up to date, look out his passport, make an appointment to have him shod about a week before you are due to go, and inspect your saddlery to ensure it's all in good repair. If your horse is kept with a sole or special companion, you may need to make additional arrangements if it is likely to become distressed at being left on its own.

Taking your horse on holiday can be a great way of exploring new areas. (Courtesy RAD Photographic)

Staying at a Riding/Trekking Centre

Taking your horse to a riding school or equestrian holiday centre is not such an expensive idea as it might seem if you were planning to put your horse in livery anyway while you are away. It gives you the chance to hack out in a new area and maybe fit in some instruction as well, but you get a break from mucking out and all the other usual chores. If holidaying with a partner or other family members, consider their interests too, and choose an area offering activities they'll enjoy while you are riding.

Research centres carefully, and visit the ones you like best to help you make the right choice; you can also discuss any special requirements your horse may have. Unless a separate paddock is available, settle for stabling rather than risking turnout with unknown horses, and make sure all your equipment is clearly marked or labelled so it is easily identified if it gets mislaid. Check in advance that the centre will be able to supply the same diet that your horse is accustomed to, as sudden changes may cause colic. If necessary, take your own feed and any special supplements he requires.

Trail Riding

If you feel more adventurous, get away from it all by taking your horse on a long distance trail ride. This can take a lot of planning, although for some people that's all part of the fun: but if it seems daunting there are companies that will do it all for you, arranging everything from route finding to emergency back-up, and transporting your baggage on ahead to pre-booked overnight stops. Arranging to go with a friend is a good idea, especially if you'll be riding in more isolated areas.

Preparation

Your horse may be travelling over terrain that is more challenging than he's used to, as well as longer distances, so it is advisable to include some longer rides of ten to fifteen miles in your fittening programme to help you assess his ability to cope. You may also need to increase or make changes to his diet: most feed manufacturers operate customer helplines where you can get advice from an equine nutritionist. And don't forget yourself: consider some extra fitness training out of the saddle, as well as spending longer in it.

Where to Stay

You can rough it and camp out if you really want to, but most riders will welcome a hot bath and a meal at night and the comfort of a soft bed, especially if the weather turns wet. It can also mean that you start each day feeling better rested and refreshed, which will obviously benefit your horse, too. If planning your own route, sort out accommodation for the horses first, using resources such as the ABRS and BHS lists of approved yards, personal recommendations from friends, the internet, Yellow Pages, riding clubs and other equine groups to help find suitable places. Once the horses are catered for, you can sort out your own arrangements.

Back-up

To avoid loading down your horses with a lot of bulky kit, a back-up crew will be needed to ferry your baggage and equipment to each overnight stop, leaving you to carry only those essentials you will need each day. They will also be able to join you at pre-arranged spots for lunch, bringing food and water for the horses. A back-up will also be able to transport all your horse's feed, so there will be no sudden changes in quality or diet at each stop: and of course if anything goes wrong and you fail to turn up they will be the first to notice and to raise the alarm. Make sure your insurance covers you for this sort of holiday, and that your back-up team is also covered.

How Far to Travel Each Day

If working out your own route, find out as much as possible in advance, using equestrian forums and contacting bridleways officers to check there are no obstructions on off-road tracks you intend to use. Specially promoted routes (see page 170, Further Information) often have printed and online guides which will make this much easier for you.

Be careful not to overestimate the distance you can comfortably cover each day. Trace the route on a map using a mapwheel measuring tool and work in either miles or kilometres – make sure you don't muddle the two as it can make a big difference. The average horse walks at a speed of between 3–4mph (5–6km/h), so to be on the comfortable side, allow one hour to travel every three miles and a little extra if travelling over very rough or hilly terrain. A distance of between fifteen to twenty miles is probably about right, allowing for the fact that although you will be walking most of the time, there are likely to be opportunities for trotting and cantering too.

Allow time in your calculations for lunch and rest breaks, and don't feel you have to spend all your time in the saddle. Dismounting and leading your horse occasionally gives his back a rest, and you the chance to stretch your legs and walk out any stiffness.

What to Take

Keep luggage to a minimum as much as possible, but remember to allow for unexpected weather changes. Comfort for your horse will be important, so take clean saddlecloths and girths, or use girth sleeves so you can slip on a clean one each day. Wearing brushing boots for extended periods every day for a week or more may cause chafing, so you

will have to weigh up whether he'd be better off without them.

If using saddlebags to carry spare clothing and other essential items, have a 'dry run' and weigh them on the bathroom scales once packed, so you can distribute the contents evenly. Accustom your horse to wearing them in a safe area at home first, and be careful to give them plenty of clearance with your right leg when mounting and dismounting.

Don't forget to pack any documentation you may need to show at his overnight accommodation, such as his passport and vaccination certificate. Also take a list of emergency contacts for vets and farriers along the way (see page 170, Further Information).

SPONSORED AND FUN RIDES

Sponsored rides often provide the opportunity of riding across land where horse riding is not normally allowed, and for those who enjoy them can lead on to endurance riding. Usually varying in length from eight to fifteen miles, many also include a variety of optional rustic-style fences set at different heights to suit all. Some rides have hundreds of riders taking part, while others are much smaller affairs: you can go by yourself, with a friend, or make up a small group, and will generally be given a riding time so that everyone sets off at regular intervals rather than as a mass start. There are no set times in which to complete the ride, so you can take things at whatever pace best suits you and your horse. A minimum amount of sponsorship money must be raised and paid in advance, although many participants simply treat it as an entry fee and sponsor themselves. As well as making a pleasant – and different – outing with your horse, these events also raise many thousands of pounds for good causes so are well worth supporting.

'Fun' rides are run along similar lines, and may or may not donate some of the profits to

Riding of the Marches in Orkney. (Courtesy Helen Foulis, Orkney Riding Club)

charity; treasure hunts are also popular, and add an extra challenge in that you have to spot clues and work out the answers to questions along the way.

Boundary Rides

Across the UK there is a growing tradition of organized rides where locals re-enact the defence of their borders from invaders or assert traditional village boundaries. Apart from enjoying the ceremony and spectacle, these can be a good way to discover new routes (although not all will be rights of way), and

meet other local riders. Examples are the Common Ridings in the Scottish Borders (see Further Information) and the Riding of the Marches in Orkney. Ask locally about such events – or you might consider establishing one in your own area as an annual get-together for the local riding community.

TREC

Trec is an acronym for Techniques de Randonnée Équestre de Compétition, and originated in France as a way of assessing the expertise of professional equestrian tourist

Trec combines elements of trail riding, orienteering, jumping, basic flatwork and handy horse classes, and tests the versatility and training of both horse and rider. (Courtesy RAD Photographic)

guides. Before long, however, leisure riders became interested in it too. Brought to the UK by the BHS in 1998, Trec has now grown into a popular form of competition with its own international governing body. Horse and rider skills are tested during three phases that take place over one or two days:

Phase One (Parcours d'Orientation et de Regularité – or POR) involves orienteering along a set route ranging from 12–45km in length.

Phase Two (Control of Paces – or CoP) tests the rider's control by first cantering and

then walking along a marked course up to 150m long and 2–4m wide. The aim is to canter as slowly as possible and walk as fast as possible without breaking gait or setting foot outside the marked area.

Phase Three (Parcours en Terrain Varié – or PTV) demonstrates the horse's obedience, confidence, courage and balance, and the rider's correct aids when tackling a number of obstacles such as steps, water, jumps, ditches, archways, bridges and gates.

There are four levels of competition, catering for beginners up to international level. Level One is the lowest, and lasts for around two to three hours, with a POR route of up to 12km and a PTV course which may include jumping obstacles up to 60cm (2ft) in height. If you feel like having a go, there are many Trec clubs that offer training and advice (*see* page 170, Further Information).

ENDURANCE RIDING

Endurance riding is becoming increasingly popular with riders of all ages and abilities. Don't imagine that it's nothing more than a long hack or gentle stroll through the countryside: part of the challenge lies in preparing and managing your horse so he finishes the ride in the best possible condition,

having covered a set route of unknown and varying terrain within a specified time. You need to be able to read and understand a map, judge speed accurately, and decide where to push on and where to ride more steadily. Although you can participate competitively, much of the pleasure comes from personal achievement and the satisfaction of a job well done. Certainly it's just as much a test of your horsemanship and stable management skills as any other equestrian discipline.

As with sponsored rides, it can be a wonderful opportunity to ride over privately owned land that you wouldn't normally have access to; and as it is also a very friendly sport you'll meet plenty of people happy to offer advice, many of whom will become new friends.

If you decide to tackle longer rides, you'll need back-up help along the way. (Courtesy RAD Photographic)

Getting Started

You don't need a lot to get started: any shape, size, type or breed of horse can take part as long as it is sound and fit enough. Your horse should be as happy to work on his own as in company, and not become anxious or overexcited about either situation. He should be confident in traffic, as routes may be partially along roads; if he's had the benefit of good basic schooling, this will help him to be relaxed and well balanced, which will be less tiring for both of you.

Your usual saddlery will be quite acceptable, although if you decide that endurance riding is for you, you may decide to invest in more specialized equipment; by this time you will probably have made plenty of friends who can advise and offer personal recommendations as to the best products to buy.

On shorter pleasure rides you should be able to cope by yourself, but as you tackle longer distances you will need a 'crew' – a partner, friend or family member who can help you prepare at the start of the ride, drive to meet you at points along the route, and assist again at the end.

The only other 'specialist' equipment that you will need you probably have already, such as rugs, sponges, buckets, water containers and 'slosh bottles' – fabric softener containers are favourite. Filled with water, these are passed up to you by your crew when they meet up with you, so that you can empty the contents over your horse's neck and body to help cool him down on warm days when he's hot and sweaty.

Classes

Most riders start by taking part in non-competitive rides (NCRs) or training rides, and these can be a good way of finding out whether endurance is a sport you enjoy and want to become more involved in. Participants generally cover distances of 16–32km (10–20 miles), travelling at an average speed of 8–12km/h (5–7½mph). If your horse is ridden three times during the week for around an hour and a half each time, he should be able to cope comfortably with the shorter distance.

If you get the taste for it, you might decide to try your hand at competitive rides (CRs), which vary in distance from 30–80km (20–50 miles) and have minimum and maximum completion times. For the ambitious and supremely fit horse and rider, endurance rides (ERs) are the toughest tests of all, covering distances of 80–160km (50–100 miles) over one or two days.

The welfare of the horse is always paramount, so there are veterinary checkpoints at the beginning and end of all competitive and endurance rides and also at points along the route for the longer rides, when there may also be compulsory rest breaks. The vetting procedure becomes increasingly more thorough as the classes become more challenging, ranging from a simple trot-up to examining for galls, cuts and sores, heart rate, hydration checks and gut sounds.

If you would like to find out more about endurance riding, get in touch with your local group – if you aren't sure who this is, contact the national governing body (*see* page 170, Further Information).

8 Problems and Emergencies

WHAT TO DO IN AN EMERGENCY

No matter how careful you are or how sensible your horse, sometimes things happen which are beyond your control. As well as making sure you have adequate insurance cover (*see* page 23, Insurance), it is therefore always best to hack out with a friend so help is immediately at hand in the event of an emergency.

No two situations are exactly the same, so although the advice given here covers a variety of different scenarios, you may need to improvise depending on the circumstances. The most important rule to remember, and the one that applies to every mishap is 'Don't panic'. If you can stay calm you will be able to think more clearly, to prioritize the actions that need to be taken, and it will have a steadying effect on others present.

Taking Action

If you are the first on the scene of an accident, try to organize whatever help is available to keep horses and any other sources of danger (such as traffic) away from casualties and to prevent them from causing any new accidents. Send for professional assistance, and treat those symptoms that, if left unattended, could result in loss of life, dealing with the most serious first. Taking first aid classes is highly recommended – you never know when you might have occasion to be grateful you made the effort to do so.

Mobile Phones

Always take a mobile phone out with you – it can be a life-saving piece of equipment in an emergency – but be sure to observe the following provisos.

- Keep the battery charged up.
- Switch the phone off or put it on silent mode while handling or riding your horse.
- If you need to make a call, always dismount first.
- Carry a list of emergency contact numbers in your pocket in case your mobile gets damaged and you can't access them.
- Carry change and a phone card in case you need to use a public phone.

Making Emergency Calls

In the UK, calling 999 will connect you to the emergency services operator. Elsewhere in the EU the emergency number is 112 (this will also work in the UK), and in the US and Canada dial 911.

Calls are free and can be made from any phone including public, mobile and car phones. If you need to contact the emergency services, speak slowly and clearly, and follow the procedures described below.

Ask for the service or services you need:

- Police.

- Fire.
- Ambulance.
- Coastguard.
- Mountain rescue.
- In the UK, should your horse become trapped, or if you come across one in need of rescue, ask for the specialist Animal Rescue team.

Provide the following information:

- Your name.
- The number you are ringing from.
- Your location: be as accurate as you can, including road names, numbers, junctions, any landmarks, and in more isolated areas the grid reference if you know it. If using a public phone your location will be displayed inside.
- The type of accident, the severity and details of any injuries, and any pre-existing medical conditions (for example epilepsy, diabetes).
- Any hazards such as weather or ground conditions so the rescue team can bring the right vehicles and equipment instead of having to send for extra tools once on the scene.

Don't hang up until the control officer has cleared the line.
If using a mobile phone:

- Leave it switched on so the emergency services can call you back.
- Put it on silent/vibrate if the ring tone is likely to alarm the horses.

If you have to leave a casualty alone in order to summon help:

- Take any vital first aid action necessary first.
- Make your call.
- Return to the injured person as quickly as possible.

- If you send another person to raise the alarm, ask them to report back to you immediately afterwards so you know that help is on its way.
- If you are in a hard-to-spot, out of the way location, use your whistle to let rescuers know where you are (*see* page 148, Lost).

Safety First

There are various measures that you can take to ensure your own safety and that of others if you are first at the scene of an emergency, and also in the course of your day-to-day riding to help prevent accidents happening:

- In an emergency situation, while waiting for help to arrive, keep yourself and others out of harm's way. A trapped or injured horse may be in a highly stressed state and, not realizing you are trying to help, can become a danger to himself and to rescuers; always be aware of your own personal safety and that of others.
- In your daily riding, particular care should be exercised when dealing with problem behaviours in a horse. These can occur as a result of any number of causes, including physical pain, poor riding, fear, diet, changes in circumstances and routine, over-confinement, lack of training, lack of experience and poor communication; moreover very often there are multiple contributory factors rather than a single one.
- Although you may need to ride positively on occasion, never resort to aggressive tactics as these are likely to increase a horse's stress levels, and also his confusion and fear, and to provoke a defensive response.
- Some behaviours can be very dangerous, and if there is no immediately apparent and easily remedied cause (such as incorrectly fitted saddlery), don't struggle on

unsuccessfully by yourself as this places you and your horse at risk, and can end up reinforcing an issue, making it more difficult to remedy. Get expert professional help – sooner rather than later – and don't risk riding out again until you have resolved the problem.

Emergency Contact Numbers

Enter emergency contact numbers on your mobile phone address book under the name ICE (In Case of Emergency). If you have more than one, enter them as ICE1, ICE2, and so on. If you are found unconscious, helpers and emergency services will know who to contact, thereby avoiding wasting precious time.

AGGRESSIVE PEOPLE

If a person approaches you in a threatening way or sexually exposes themselves to you, remove yourself from the immediate area as quickly but calmly as possible. Do not get involved in trading insults, as this may inflame the situation. Avoid direct eye contact, and keep your distance – do not get close enough for the person to grab hold of your horse's reins. If the offender is driving a car, lorry or motorcycle, move off the road if necessary for your own safety, and try to memorize the number plate if possible. Once safely out of harm's way, contact the police and report the incident to them.

BOLTING

Care should always be taken when cantering or galloping in company – some horses may get overexcited or anxious about being left behind and will become very strong, ignoring the rider as they try to remain close to their equine

---

NOTES FOR RIDE ESCORTS

On returning to the stables, make out a report in the Accident/Incident Book while everything is fresh in your mind: include near misses as well as those accidents resulting in obvious injury. Take statements from other riders who were witnesses to the accident. The insurance company and your local authority Environmental Health Officer should be notified of any injury to a person, or damage to property, motor vehicle or the like, which could result in a claim.

---

companions. Try to not always canter or gallop in the same places, as your horse may begin to anticipate it.

It can be alarming enough trying to control a horse which is going faster than you want, but it is even more frightening if he has gone into a blind panic and a true bolt, making him even harder to stop. Flight is a basic survival tactic, and although training helps to overcome this innate instinct, it can still sometimes surface unexpectedly. Even the best behaved and quietest horse can become frightened by something unusual, causing him to spook or run away. Pain can also be a cause of bolting, whether from an insect bite or sting, poor riding, ill-fitting saddlery, or a physical problem. Teeth are often neglected and get left off the 'to check' list, but should be examined by a vet or equine dental technician at least once a year.

If you feel your horse beginning to get strong you might try the following tactics in order to retain control:

● Ask him to return to walk.
● Use your voice to reassure and relax him. Do not shout.

Be careful not to let things get out of control when galloping in company. (Courtesy RAD Photographic)

- Ask for some lateral flexion as this will make it harder for him to set his jaw against you and run forwards.
- Transitions between walk and a gentle jog trot may help to keep him between hand and leg, but be tactful with your aids.
- With a horse that has a tendency to become strong, teaching him to work with a TTEAM Balance Rein (*see* page 137, Breakages) can be helpful: because it encourages softening and relaxation of the muscles on the underside of the neck he'll be less inclined to brace through it, and it can also help discourage him from leaning or fixing against the hand.

If you lose control:

- Do not attempt to jump off unless it is absolutely imperative because it is difficult to throw yourself clear when travelling at speed and you will hit the ground very hard indeed.
- Do not point your horse towards a fence, wall or other solid barrier as he may attempt to jump it or run head first into it.

- Do not scream or shout as this may scare him into going faster still.
- Get yourself in a secure position, with your heels deep. Bring your body into an upright position: if your horse puts his head down low, brace one hand on the base of his neck so he is pulling against himself, and cannot pull you forward. If his head is high, doing this may also help to keep it more stable and the bit to act on the bars of the mouth instead of being pulled up against the back teeth.
- Give a few short sharp tugs on the other rein, releasing the pressure between each tug, then brace that hand on the neck and take tugs on the opposite rein. Take care not to pull the horse off balance and over on to his side.
- If tugs on the reins seem to be having little effect, try a side-to-side sawing movement instead.
- If you have enough space, fix one hand to the inside to bring the horse round in a big circle. However, you will need to take care not to pull him over sideways, and in practice there is rarely sufficient room for this sort of manoeuvre.

If someone else loses control:

- Do not gallop after them, as the sound of your pursuit may make their horse go even faster.
- Follow on at a steady trot until you catch up.

Finding a Solution

The most usual recourse with a horse that gets strong is to try successively stronger bits. This may be the solution – better to use a more severe bit with tact than to haul at the horse's mouth and rely on brute strength for control. But it is not always the answer: a severe bit can also frighten the horse, and cause it to fight the contact or try and run from the pain (especially in the hands of a rough rider). Don't rule out the possibility that a milder bit, or even a bitless bridle, might be more successful.

You should also always check for any physical problems or injuries, address schooling, try to avoid putting the horse in overexciting situations, and ensure a correct food-to-exercise ratio and adequate turnout time.

- Always try out a different bit in a safe enclosed environment at home before using it out hacking.

BREAKAGES

Broken Stirrup Leather

Hold the mane or neckstrap to help you keep your balance. If you have a spare leather with you, replace it, but continue in walk in case the other one is in a similar condition to the broken one. If you don't have a spare, lead your horse home or arrange for transport home: do not ride without stirrups, as this will reduce your security in the event of your horse shying or misbehaving in some way.

- Practise riding at home in a safe, enclosed environment without stirrups, starting in walk and progressing to faster gaits as you gain in confidence and security, so you will be less alarmed if you lose a stirrup or the leather breaks.

Broken Girth Strap

If a girth strap breaks while you are out, carefully inspect the remaining two to assess their soundness; only if you are satisfied with their condition should you attach the girth to them. You should then make your way home at walk. If you have any doubts as to the safety of the remaining straps, or if your saddle only had two girth straps, lead your horse or arrange for transport. Never attempt to ride on a single girth strap.

Broken Rein

If a rein breaks while you are mounted but standing still, jump off immediately. If the horse is moving, give a series of slowing aids with the unbroken rein, but remember that the one-sided application will tend to turn him in that direction too. It may be possible to reach forward with your hand to take hold of the section of broken rein: take a handful of mane with the other hand to support yourself as you do so, and keep your heels deep.

You can also use a verbal command to encourage him to slow down – if he is used to being lunged this can work well – and if you have a neckstrap, use it to give quick tug-and-release signals in an upward direction. If you have taught him to work in a TTEAM Balance Rein (*see overleaf*) it will be easy to slow and halt him without the bridle reins. Wait until he has either stopped or is going slowly enough for you to judge that you can safely jump off (*see* page 145, Emergency Dismount).

The TTEAM Balance Rein

The TTEAM Balance Rein is a simple and effective way of teaching your horse how to balance himself more correctly, and can act as an emergency 'brake' should you need one.

The light pressure applied by the Balance Rein to the base of the horse's neck can help trigger the 'seeking reflex', which encourages the withers to lift and the neck to lengthen from withers to poll. It helps with horses that tend to brace through the neck, and teaches them how to transfer weight off the forehand and back through the body; it is therefore a great help for those that tend to be 'downhill' and inclined to lean on the hand or stumble as a result. It is equally useful with horses that jog or have a high head carriage, and can help when teaching your horse to move backwards, and also with horses inclined to shy, because they learn to slow down and listen more to their rider.

Introducing and Using the TTEAM Balance Rein

The Balance Rein is a loop of rope which hangs round the horse's neck; it is possible to improvise with a length of half-inch diameter rope, or you can buy a purpose-made one with a rope section incorporated into a leather rein,

Introduce the Balance Rein from the ground. (Bob Atkins, courtesy Horse & Rider *magazine)*

The person leading will need to co-ordinate their actions with those of the person holding the Balance Rein. (Bob Atkins, courtesy Horse & Rider *magazine)*

which makes it easier to hold. The round profile of rope works better than the flat surface of an old stirrup leather or rein; if you use a leadrope, cut the clip off first, for safety.

Always introduce this work in a safe enclosed area, and start by working from the ground. You will need the help of another person initially.

- Begin with one of you leading, while the other person walks alongside the horse holding one end of the Balance Rein in each hand as it hangs around his neck. Make sure it hangs loosely while he is moving.

- Ask for halt by giving a gentle signal on the Balance Rein in an upward and diagonal direction, following the line of the horse's shoulder. Take care not to pull sideways, as this can cause the horse to become laterally unbalanced.

- Immediately after signalling on the Balance Rein, release the tension so it hangs slack again – it is on this release that the horse will slow or stop. Don't keep up a constant pull, as this will cause the horse to lean against it. If he takes no notice, try a slightly firmer upward signal followed by the release: if necessary the person leading can help cue

Once ready to try ridden work, ask your assistant to walk beside you in case you need help.
(Bob Atkins, courtesy **Horse & Rider** *magazine)*

the halt. Remember that for the horse, it's a new feeling and way of organizing his body, which he may find physically and mentally challenging, so be patient.

● Once the horse halts in response to a signal on the Balance Rein alone you can move on to ridden work. Secure the ends of the balance rein so it forms a continuous loop round the horse's neck. Hold the bridle reins as usual, and the Balance Rein so it passes between the second and third fingers of each hand: keeping them separate and spaced apart makes it easier for you to differentiate between the two.

● Ask someone to walk alongside when you start ridden work, just in case you get into difficulties. Begin as before, asking the horse to walk a few steps and keeping the Balance Rein slack, then halting using the same 'ask-and-release' signal as before. Ride frequent transitions between walk and halt. Each time you use the Balance Rein to stop, the horse will be learning how to lighten his forehand and becoming straighter, squarer and engaging his hindquarters more strongly.

- When the walk and halt work is established, introduce some trot; just a few steps initially and then ask for a downward transition to walk. If you've prepared thoroughly enough with the earlier work, you won't find this difficult. As the horse is being asked to lengthen his neck, you may need to allow him more rein than previously.

- Gradually try using the Balance Rein in more subtle ways, to help slow and steady, so the horse learns how to improve his balance while in movement as well as during transitions. The proportional contact between Balance Rein and bridle rein can vary as needed: it can be 50:50 or 60:40 or 40:60 – if he pulls or leans against the bit, have more contact on the Balance Rein. Remember that it is important not to keep up a steady tension on it, as this will invite the horse to lean against it, and that the rebalance comes on the 'release', not the 'ask' part of your signal on it.

- Spread this work over several sessions, and bear in mind that some horses learn more quickly than others. You do not have to hold the Balance Rein the whole time while out hacking if you don't want to – leave it lying on your horse's neck and just pick it up when you need to use it.

Practise transitions between walk and halt before progressing to halt.
(Bob Atkins, courtesy Horse & Rider *magazine)*

BUCKING

Horses sometimes buck through high spirits and exuberance, but if it happens regularly, discomfort is more likely to be the cause, whether from an ill-fitting saddle, back pain, teeth, bit, feet and legs, or the rider.

- Arrange to have your horse, his saddlery and your own riding thoroughly checked over.
- Ensure the horse is not over-confined, but turned out for as long as possible every day, and feed according to his workload.
- Avoid putting him in situations that might require you to over-contain him with the rein contact, or that are likely to trigger a panic response, such as galloping in company.
- Horseflies and warble flies can madden some horses, so use an effective repellent during the summer months.

Signs that a horse might be about to buck include lowering his head and hunching or rounding up his back, and tightly clamping down his tail. You may be able to pre-empt bucking by asking him to move forwards actively but steadily; it may also help to ask for some flexion, or to ride shoulder-in or a small circle.

If he does buck, keep your heels deep, and your knees, ankle and hip joints flexed so they work effectively as shock absorbers. Look up and ahead to help you balance better, and maintain a positive rein contact, trying to keep the horse's head up and to ride him forwards into it.

FALLING OFF

Inevitably at some point in your riding career you will fall off, even though safe and sensible riding practice reduces the risk of this happening. If, however, you reach the point of no return and falling off becomes inevitable, try to minimize injury by adopting the following tactics.

- Relax.
- Tuck your head into your shoulder and pull your arms and legs in towards your body to help protect limbs and internal organs.
- Try to roll away from your horse's hooves as you curl up.
- Let go of the reins: if you keep hold of them you risk being dragged by your horse, which may tread on you or kick out at you in fear. It also increases the likelihood of fractures and dislocations.
- Remain on the ground in your curled position until any following horses have passed or stopped; if you try to get up immediately they may find it hard to avoid you, and will knock you down again.

This advice is not always easy to follow, as it is hard to override the instinct to brace yourself or to put out a hand. It's worth enquiring whether your riding school offers any tuition in the art of falling off, so you can practise doing it correctly. Protective clothing can help minimize injuries (*see* page 25, What to Wear), and teaching the 'Sliding Saddlecloth' exercise can be helpful (*see* page 145).

Whether you remount and continue your ride after a fall depends on a number of factors, including the reason for the fall, whether you or your horse are injured, and whether the saddlery is sound and safe to use. Never allow anyone with suspected concussion (which can occur without the rider having been unconscious) or other head injuries to remount.

If you are in any doubt as to the advisability of remounting, then don't. The traditional advice about getting back on again immediately isn't always wise, and may be safer to do in an enclosed area with an experienced and sympathetic instructor on hand.

First Aid in the Event of a Rider Fall

All riders should make the effort to attend some first aid training, as it will help you make the right decisions in an emergency, and could save lives. In the event of a rider falling off, it is essential to observe the following code of practice.

- Stay calm.
- Make the area safe if necessary to prevent you, the casualty and others coming to further harm.
- Go quietly to the injured person: if they are conscious, tell them to remain still.
- Ask if there is pain in any particular area; if there is pain, or they cannot move their fingers and/or toes, on no account move them before skilled help arrives.
- Alert the emergency services as quickly as possible. As well as sending help, they will be able to advise as to care of the casualty.
- Keep the casualty warm: cover them with a coat or blanket.
- Keep talking to reassure them.
- *Do not* leave the casualty alone, unless there is no one else present who can go for help.
- *Do not* remove their riding hat.
- *Do not* offer food, drinks or cigarettes.

NOTES FOR RIDE ESCORTS

- All incidents – even when the rider seems unhurt – should be recorded in the yard accident/incident book, and statements taken from any riders who witnessed it.
- At least one ride escort should possess a current recognized first aid qualification, and it is recommended that ride escorts attend first aid refresher courses.
- Always carry a pocket first aid kit.

In the event of all but the most minor impact the rider's riding hat and body protector should be replaced (*see* page 25, What to Wear).

FOOT CAUGHT OVER THE REIN

Horses sometimes manage to get a foot caught over the rein, usually when they put their head down to graze. If this happens while you are mounted, jump off immediately you notice what has happened. Keep hold of the reins, and quietly and calmly unbuckle them to release them from around his leg.

If the horse is treading on the rein you will need to lift his foot, but if he is pulling against the self-imposed restraint, this may be difficult – try leaning slightly against his shoulder as you do so. Be aware that as he feels the pressure on his mouth released he may rear up, so be careful. Check for damage to his mouth and to the bridlework.

HORSE FALLS

Your horse might fall for any number of reasons, including putting a foot down a pothole, tripping on uneven ground, or due to an injury or other physical problem. Take special care when riding across slippery and loose surfaces (*see* page 63, Slippery Surfaces and Loose Surfaces): if they can't be avoided, consider whether it might be safest to dismount and lead him until you reach better ground. It is not always a preventable occurrence, however, and if your horse falls while travelling at speed, with luck you'll be thrown clear. Should you be going more slowly, or if your horse is at risk of falling due to insecure footing, it's worth knowing how to do an emergency dismount (*see* page 145).

Sliding Saddlecloth Exercise

This TTEAM exercise is excellent for helping horses that are easily startled by sudden movement, or nervous about things touching their sides, as may happen while out hacking. It is also useful to teach in case you have a fall, as your horse will learn to stop calmly rather than kick out or run off in panic when he feels something sliding down his sides.

● Ask someone to hold your horse while you place a saddlecloth on his back, and then slowly slide it off to the side, keeping hold

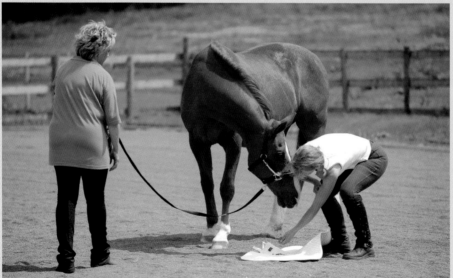

TOP: Introduce the exercise while your horse is in halt. (Bob Atkins, courtesy Horse & Rider *magazine)*

BELOW: Use food to help develop a positive association with the saddlecloth. (Bob Atkins, courtesy Horse & Rider *magazine)*

of it as you do so. If he's concerned about this, use a small pad, building up to a full size saddlecloth as his confidence grows. Let him inspect it if he wants: this exercise is about developing his confidence, not about forcing him to stand still while you do things to him. Put a little food on it to create a positive association with it.

- When he is relaxed about this, slowly slide the saddlecloth off towards you again, but this time let it fall to the ground. Quickly place some food on it, guiding his head to it if necessary as he may not realize at first that it's there. Stay on the same side as your assistant in case your horse swings his body away from the moving saddlecloth.
- Once he is confident with this, ask your assistant to lead him forwards while you walk alongside holding the saddlecloth in place with one hand. As before, slowly slide it off to the side, allow it to drop to the floor, and place some treats on it: the moment this happens your assistant asks your horse to halt – you'll need to communicate clearly with her about what you are doing, so she knows when to ask him to stop.
- Most horses learn very quickly that when they feel the saddlecloth sliding off, if they stop it is actually a rewarding experience, and not a frightening one. Do the exercise on both sides, and also practise drawing the cloth off over the quarters.
- Once your horse has learned the exercise thoroughly, use variable reinforcement: this is when the food reward arrives unpredictably, on the second, third or fourth repetition rather than every time. This encourages your horse to think about what he is doing, instead of focusing only on the food – but be lavish with your praise each time.

Check your horse over carefully afterwards: he may be winded, so speak to him reassuringly and allow him to get to his feet in his own time. Once he's up, look for any signs of injury or lameness, and use your common sense to decide whether to continue on your way, or to return home, or call for assistance. If you have no idea as to why he fell, either lead or transport him home and ask your vet to examine him to eliminate any possibility of a physical problem.

NOTES FOR RIDE LEADERS

If teaching clients how to do an emergency dismount, do so only in a safe, enclosed environment, preferably on a yielding surface such as that of a manège or school, and ensure they are wearing a body protector and hard hat. Have a portable mounting block nearby for remounting.

- The horse must be quiet and held on a leading rein: keep a close eye on it throughout, and stop if it shows any signs of restlessness or concern.
- Demonstrate how to do an emergency dismount, and then allow the client to practise, first of all from halt. Only progress to trying it in walk when the client is both competent and confident while the horse is standing still.
- When successful in walk, try from a slow trot if the client wishes to do so.

An Emergency Dismount

- Take both feet out of the stirrups.
- Let go of the reins and place both hands on the withers, just in front of the saddle.

- Lean forwards, and if dismounting off the near (left) side of the horse, swing your right leg over his back. Use your hands as well as the momentum of your upper body to help you vault off and to push you away from the horse.
- Bend your knees as you land to help you balance and to absorb the shock of landing. If you do fall over, roll away from the horse.
- *Do not* wrap your arms around your horse's neck, as you will be at risk of swinging round in front of him where you may get trampled, or may bring him down on top of you; you will also be interfering badly with his already compromised balance, and could injure his neck.

INDISCRIMINATE GRAZING

Young children often don't have the strength or speed of reaction to stop ponies from putting their heads down to graze – and occasionally novice adult riders find themselves struggling,

too. The reins may actually be jerked right out of the rider's hands – or if a tight grip is kept on them, the rider will be pulled forwards, sometimes right out of the saddle. As well as being annoying, this can be frightening for novices and young children, and is a potentially dangerous habit.

Often the advice given is to bridge the reins and ride forwards positively, but this will only work if the rider has a sufficient degree of anticipation, quick reflexes and good co-ordination, which most children and inexperienced riders don't have. If this is the case, use either grass reins or a daisy rein to prevent this happening.

Grass reins run from the bit cheekpieces, up the side of the face, through the loops at each end of the browband, and then back to attach to the front saddle Ds. A daisy rein attaches to the bridle headpiece and fastens to the front of the saddle. Both can be bought from saddlery retailers, or in an emergency you can improvise with a length of twine, using quick release knots.

Daisy rein.

Grass rein.

The reins should be adjusted so as to allow the horse a comfortable natural head carriage and so he can flex laterally, but should be short enough to prevent his head reaching the ground. Side reins are best avoided as he could risk catching a foot through them.

JOGGING AND SNATCHING AT THE REINS

This is a tiring and uncomfortable habit for both horse and rider; not all horses that jog snatch at the reins, but the two often go together. The possible causes, and how you might deal with them, include the following:

- Overfreshness: try to arrange more turnout time. As well as having no outlet to use up their physical energy, horses stabled for long periods will invariably be more keyed up mentally, increasing the likelihood of jogging.
- Overfeeding: reduce the concentrate ration and increase the forage.
- Feeling cold in winter: if your horse is clipped, try using an exercise blanket.
- Weather: windy conditions, driving rain or both may cause jogging. Try using a rain sheet or exercise blanket, making sure it has a fillet string to keep it from blowing up: he may settle after a spell of steady trot work.
- Discomfort: this may be caused by sharp teeth, bitting, saddlery or other physical problems. Rider stiffness, or gripping with the legs, rough hands and an over-restrictive rein contact may also be responsible.
- Separation anxiety: a shorter-striding horse may jog to try and keep up with those ahead. Teach him how to lengthen his stride, and ask the one at the front to shorten his, so their gait speeds match better; alternatively find a better suited hacking companion. (*See also* page 157, Separation Anxiety.)

- Excitable when with other horses: try to work on schooling at home with other horses, so he learns that their presence isn't always exciting, and to focus on you instead.
- Poor balance, especially horses with a high headcarriage: spend time on schooling to help remedy this, and encourage him to work between leg and hand.
- Fatigue: a tired horse will have a more erratic headcarriage, and will be likely to snatch at the reins in order to stretch his head and neck.

Teaching your horse to work with a TTEAM balance rein can be a great help with horses that jog: *see* page 138 for details.

LAME HORSE

The lameness may be mild, showing as a slight unevenness in gait, or severe, with your horse maybe coming to an abrupt standstill or very obviously hobbling along. The moment you notice something is wrong, stop, dismount, and check the leg you suspect. If you can't find anything wrong, check the other three in case you have mistaken which is the lame leg.

The most common cause of lameness while out hacking is picking up a stone or bruising the sole, so lift up the foot and clean it out. If a stone is responsible, your horse will usually go sound again once it is removed. If an object such as a nail has penetrated the foot, keep the horse as still as possible and phone for veterinary assistance. It may be necessary to remove the object – if you have the tools to do so with you – to prevent it from being driven in even deeper as your horse puts his foot down, in which case note the place, angle and depth of penetration. Veterinary attention is essential, because even though it may not look serious once the object is withdrawn, there is a risk that structures within the foot may be involved.

If your horse goes lame you may need to lead him home if you are close enough, or arrange for transport to collect you. (Courtesy RAD Photographic)

If he is lame due to a serious wound (*see* page 169, Wounds), has a suspected fracture, or is otherwise unable to put weight on the foot, keep him as quiet as possible and call the vet as a matter of urgency.

Do not try and ride your horse if he is lame, even if the lameness is mild: you may make matters worse, and it is also unsafe as he may be more likely to stumble or fall. If you are close to home, lead him back on foot, though be ready to stop if the lameness appears to be getting worse. If the horse is obviously lame in walk, this indicates that he is very lame, and you should call for assistance to transport him home.

LOST

Carry a map and compass when riding in unfamiliar areas (and know how to use both), as this can prevent you from getting lost in the first place. Before you leave the yard make sure someone knows where you've gone, and when you expect to return or arrive at your destination, so that if you don't turn up a search can be organized.

Getting lost in an urban or cultivated rural area is not a major problem: inquiring at shops, farms and country pubs, or asking pedestrians, should get you pointed in the right direction again – although do exercise caution when approaching strangers. If you see a public telephone box there may be information inside that will help you pinpoint your location. If all else fails, you can retrace your footsteps again.

If you go astray in a more isolated spot, things may be more difficult. The moment you realize you are lost, observe the following code of practice:

- Stay calm and stop.
- Look at your map if you have one with you, and compare it with your surroundings: you may be able to work out where you are after all, and to find your way from there. You may get a better view from the summit of a hill, but don't go miles to go up one. If you can clearly identify your hoofmarks, consider retracing your steps until you know where you are.
- Call for help on your mobile phone: pass on any relevant information about your surroundings, which will give searchers some idea of where to look for you. If you can't get a signal on your mobile phone, you'll be glad you thought to tell someone where you were going.
- If you are with a friend, stay together – don't split up except in very exceptional circumstances.
- Stay in one place. Moving around will make it harder for rescuers to find you: you could be going in the wrong direction, or even round in circles, and will be exhausting your horse needlessly. If it's getting dark, misty or foggy, it could be dangerous too, as you won't be able to see where you're going.
- Cover any exposed skin. If it's hot this will help prevent sunburn, and if it's cold it will help keep you warm. Shelter out of wind and rain if cover is available, but not where searchers won't be able to see you.
- Spread out something bright and easily visible from a distance – use hi-vis clothing as a flag,

or spread it out on the ground, weighed down with rocks so it doesn't blow away.
- Make a noise! Use your whistle, as the sound carries better than your voice and is less tiring: six sharp blasts repeated at minute intervals is the international distress signal, or three in the US and Canada, but trained rescuers will be familiar with both. If you hear a response, keep blowing until you have made visual contact.

LOOSE HORSE

If you fall off your horse or he gets loose during a break, take care when going to catch him, as he may behave differently than when at home. If he is loose because something scared him, his adrenalin levels will be high, and even if he is normally easy to catch, you may find he is spooky and wary. If the saddle has slipped around his side or the irons are flapping, it can also frighten him and cause him to act unpredictably and explosively.

Approach slowly and quietly, using a soothing voice to calm and reassure him. If you move up to him sideways on this is less threatening than if you march up facing full on to him. If you have some food, use it to encourage him to approach you as you get closer – but if you don't, the old joke about catching a horse by making a noise like a carrot isn't entirely silly: rustling a bag or pretending to pull a treat out of a pocket, even if it's only a hanky, may do the trick.

If you're with other riders, ask them to stay together and hopefully your horse's herd instinct will override his anxieties and he'll want to stay near his friends. If he is wary of you, ask one of the riders to lead their horse beside you, as this may overcome any apprehension and enable you to get close enough to catch him. If he keeps moving off when you get within a certain distance, try walking away, as he may follow rather than being left on his own.

If you fall off and your horse gets loose he may be spookier than usual. (Courtesy RAD Photographic)

If he is on the road and you cannot catch him straightaway, or if he gallops off towards a road, contact the police immediately so they can warn and halt traffic where necessary, as he will be a hazard to road users as well as himself. If you are with other riders, ask someone to control the traffic until police assistance arrives (*see also* page 156, Road Accident).

Should you be in isolated countryside and he gallops off, follow him to the point where you lose sight of him, and then mark the area physically and on your map: but don't get lost yourself. Summon help, and search parties can be organized to comb the area, fanning out from that point. Notify any yards in the area as well as police, in case he is caught by someone else.

Your horse should have some form of ID on him (*see* page 39, What to Take with You) so that if a stranger catches him you can be contacted. Teaching the TTEAM 'Sliding Saddlecloth' exercise (*see* page 144) can also help prevent the whole scenario from arising in the first place.

● If you are riding on MoD land, don't leave the route to go after him if you part company, but contact the relevant site operator.

LOST SHOE

Loose shoes are more likely to come off, but deep going can cause even a newly shod horse to pull off a shoe, or if the toe of a hind shoe catches the heel of a front one. The moment you realize there is a problem, find a place where you can safely dismount and check your horse's foot. If the shoe is just slightly loose and you aren't too far from home you may be able to walk or lead him back; but if it has twisted you will need to ring for help so you can remove the shoe to prevent it from causing injury or damaging the hoof.

If the shoe has been lost altogether, either walk or lead the horse home using soft verges wherever possible to minimize damage to the hoof itself. On longer rides where you may be some distance from home, carry a hoofboot of some kind to protect the foot in such eventualities, until the permanent shoe can be replaced.

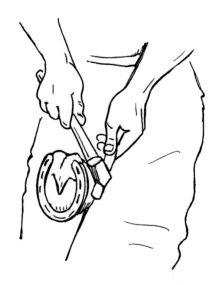

Use hammer and buffer to knock up the clenches.

Removing a shoe looks easy when the farrier does it – ask him to show you and let you do a couple under his supervision.

Removing a Shoe

It is possible to improvise, but having the right tools makes the job of taking off a shoe much easier, and you will be less likely to damage the foot. These tools include a hammer, buffer, rasp and pincers – and it makes a big difference if you keep the buffer sharp.

- To remove a shoe from a front foot, face towards the horse's quarters, pick up the foot and place it between your legs just above your knees. Keep your knees pressed close together, turning your toes inwards slightly to help. If the shoe is on a back foot, face towards the rear, pick the foot up and support it along your inside thigh.
- Knock up all the clenches by setting the blade of the buffer under each one in turn and giving it a couple of sharp blows with the hammer. If you find this difficult, try rasping over the clenches, using the smoother side of the rasp, to remove them instead.

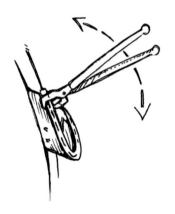

TOP LEFT: Use the pincers to lever the heels of the shoe upwards.

TOP RIGHT: Knock the shoe back down, leaving the nail heads proud, and use pincers to draw each nail out.

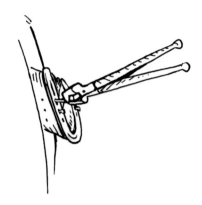

LEFT: Shoeing tools. From left: pincers, hammer, buffer and rasp.

● Once all the clenches have been either straightened out or rasped off, close the pincers around one heel of the shoe and lever it in an upward and forward direction towards the toe. As the shoe is lifted away from the hoof the head of the nail will move with it. Tap the shoe back down on to the foot, leaving the nail head proud. Take hold of it with the pincers and lever the nail out. Repeat the process with the opposite shoe heel, and continue in this way working towards the toe.

● When you get to the last two nails it should be possible to pull them out and lift off the shoe all together by placing the pincers under the shoe and drawing them upwards and backwards towards the frog. Once off, if you have a hoof boot, use it to help protect the hoof wall until the hoof can be reshod.

Removing a shoe looks easier than it is, so when your farrier next calls, ask him to demonstrate and allow you to take off a shoe or two so you are confident and competent enough to cope in an emergency.

- A word of advice: protect your legs – leather chaps work well.

MEETING DOGS

Accustom your horse to dogs as much as possible, so that should you meet one out on a ride he is less likely to be alarmed by it. Although it is the safest thing to do, there is no legal requirement for an owner to put their dog on a lead when passing horses. While responsible owners will do so when they see you approaching, others are less considerate. Worryingly, actual attacks are on the increase and have resulted in serious injuries to both horses and riders: should this happen to you, notify the police and the local dog warden following the incident.

Politely ask the owner to put a loose dog on the leash, keeping your horse in halt while they do so – movement will excite the dog further, increase any desire to chase, and make it harder for the owner to catch it. Once the owner has done that – or if the dog was on a lead anyway – remember to smile and thank them.

If the dog is unaccompanied, allow your horse to turn to face the dog if he wishes, so he can see it clearly. Although you may be feeling anxious, don't shout at the dog. Like horses, many dog behaviours are motivated by fear, so becoming more aggressive and threatening may inflame the situation. However, it may be worth saying 'Sit!' in a firm, authoritative voice, as this is one of the commands that most dogs do know.

Dogs are often a feature on farms, but the landowner has a duty to make sure they do not injure or intimidate path users. Whether the law has been broken depends on the circumstances of each case: report the matter to the local council and see what they think.

- Some riding clubs run demonstrations at local dog shows and training classes to encourage dog owners to socialize their pets, and to help them better understand how to be safe around horses. Suggest this to your local riding club, particularly if problems are increasing in your area.

Riding with your Dog

It is not advisable to let your dog accompany you on rides with your horse. If he gets too close to your horse or startles him, he may get kicked or trodden on, or cause other horses that are edgy around dogs to panic. Also your attention will be constantly divided between your horse and the need to keep an eye on your dog, and if anything happens you will not be able to intervene as quickly as when on foot, and may be hampered by the need to keep hold of your horse. In certain areas leash laws may be in force, and being on horseback is no excuse for not picking up after your dog, both in law and out of courtesy.

NAPPING

A nappy horse will come to a standstill and refuse to continue forwards: if pressurized by the rider to continue he may keep his feet planted, or try to run backwards, spin round and attempt to go back in the direction he's just come from, buck or even rear.

It may be considered that in behaving like this he is being naughty and awkward, but often this is simply another form of shying or spooking, and can be due to lack of confidence or fear (*see* page 159, Shying and Spooking, and page 157, Separation Anxiety). If turned round to face towards home he may speed up – sometimes faster and with less control than you'd like – in his desire to get away from whatever he perceives to be scary, and to get back home, where he feels safer.

If your horse does nap, it is a mistake to kick or hit him, because using this sort of pressure increases his stress levels even more and he won't be thinking at all, just reacting, possibly dangerously for both of you. Calm him and reassure him, and after a moment or two he may be prepared to go forwards again. If you are with another horse, ask its rider to give you a lead.

If yours remains 'stuck', try moving both hands a little to the side to swing his shoulders slightly sideways and help get his feet moving again; or dismount and lead him. Use your voice, but be encouraging rather than shouting at him.

If your horse naps persistently, he obviously isn't enjoying going out, and you should ask yourself why not. Points to consider include the following:

Pain/discomfort: Physical pain, or discomfort caused by saddlery or the rider should always be investigated as a potential cause. Horses can sometimes be very stoic and will tolerate quite considerable discomfort for some time before finally being unable to endure it any longer.

Lack of confidence: The company of a steady and experienced horse can be a great confidence booster. You can also try some 'confidence training' at home (*see* page 87, Confidence Training), when trust in the rider can also be developed.

Fear: Your horse may be genuinely fearful of something, even though you may not notice anything out of the ordinary. Equine senses of smell and hearing are much better than ours, and they also tend to be cautious of anything unfamiliar. This applies not just to tangible objects, but also when things that are usually in a certain place are not there any longer, or if they have been moved to a different place.

Vision: The horse is highly sensitive to movement but unable to focus quickly on objects, so he may be inclined either to keep his distance from something he finds scary, or to run away from it until he knows it is safe; deterioration in vision can also be responsible for problems.

Habit: Choosing a circular route is preferable wherever possible: if you always retrace your footsteps on a linear ride it can become an established habit and your horse may show reluctance when you then try to vary the routine in any way. Where there is no choice, try to use schooling exercises (*see* page 116, Schooling) where it is safe to do so, and vary the distance travelled each time, so no two rides are absolutely identical.

Fatigue: Becoming physically overtired can also be a cause of napping, something which is easily overlooked.

REARING

A horse may resort to rearing if it is asked to go forwards and is unable or afraid to do so, and is prevented from moving in any other direction. If your horse does rear, incline your upper body forwards so you stay in balance with him: don't pull on the reins but use the mane for support if necessary. Take both feet out of the stirrups so you can slide off quickly if he does more than lift his front feet a little way off the ground and begins to really go up, when there may be a danger of him losing his footing and coming over on top of you.

Make sure that you are not using over-strong rein aids or over-severe bitting which is inhibiting forward movement. Even a mild bit can cause a great deal of discomfort if it is the wrong size or incorrectly adjusted: ask someone to check, and also have your horse's mouth looked over by a vet or an equine dental

Push the thumbpiece on each stirrup bar into the down position so it lies horizontal. This enables the stirrup leather to slide off in the event of a fall, and if your foot is trapped in a stirrup. If the saddle has a closed D-ring attachment for stirrup leathers (often seen on treeless saddles), use safety stirrups or Barnes buckles which will release the stirrup from the leather if the rider falls and gets a foot trapped.

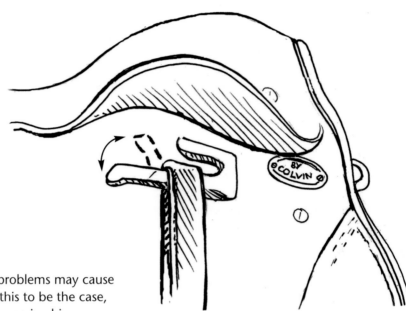

technician. Other physical problems may cause rearing, and if you suspect this to be the case, ask your vet to thoroughly examine him.

If he is rearing because he is being confronted with something he finds scary, don't force issues: in the short term, reassure him, get another horse to give him a lead, or if appropriate and safe to do so, try leading him on foot or using food as a lure. In the long term aim to build up his confidence and develop his trust in you (*see also* page 153, Napping, and page 87, Confidence Training).

RIDER DRAGGED BEHIND THEIR HORSE

A rider falling off and then being dragged because their foot is caught in the stirrup is one of the most horrific events to witness as there is little you can do, and it can result in serious injury or even prove fatal. If the rider fell due to the horse being scared by something, it may try to flee from the cause of its fear; a trapped rider being dragged along may frighten it even more, making it buck and kick out in an attempt to get rid of this additional terrifying object.

Chasing after the horse may make matters worse. Your best course of action is to follow at a quiet pace and hope that the horse will slow down as it realizes it is alone, and because it will want to rejoin your own horse – or that the rider's foot becomes free, or that the horse either stops of its own accord or is stopped by someone ahead of it.

Prevention is always the best policy: at the very least, check that the thumbpieces on the stirrup bars are in the 'down' position, that footwear is appropriate, stirrup irons the right width, and foot placement in the irons is correct. Never ride with the feet pushed through the leathers above the irons, and if you don't already have them, consider buying safety irons, toe cages, Barnes buckles or such safety items that aim either to prevent the feet getting trapped or to release them immediately in the event of a fall.

Teaching the TTEAM 'Sliding Saddlecloth' exercise (*see* page 144) is also invaluable.

ROAD ACCIDENTS

If you are on the scene of a road traffic accident involving a horse, immediate action is necessary: you can't do everything yourself, so recruit the help of motorists, other road users and pedestrians to assist with directing traffic, catching and holding loose horses, treating any casualties, and ringing the emergency services.

While waiting for professional help to arrive, set up warning points 200m (250 yards) to the front and rear of the accident area. The ignition of any vehicles damaged in the accident should be switched off, and also the fuel supply of motorcycles.

Any injured horses should be moved to the side or off the road if possible, unless they are down and unwilling or unable to rise, in which case do not try and force them to get up. If a horse is thrashing around in an attempt to get to his feet but is very obviously unable to do so, you may need to restrain him to prevent him from injuring himself further. You can do this by kneeling on his neck just behind his head from the spine side, where you won't put pressure on the windpipe and are clear of the front feet. Covering the eyes with a jacket or fleece may also help. (*See also* page 142, Falling Off.)

Making Out an Accident Report

If you are involved in, or witness, or know of an accident (or near miss) involving a horse on the road, you should fill in a BHS accident report form (*see* page 170, Further Information). At the moment, such incidents don't have to be reported to police unless the rider needs medical help. The horse can even be fatally injured without the incident being investigated or reported to the police. This makes it difficult to collate statistics, which could then be used to help make roads safer places for horse riders, and to promote alternative off-road routes.

NOTES FOR RIDE LEADERS

In the event of an accident, keep calm, and keep control: halt your ride in an orderly manner, ask them all to dismount and move off the road, or to the side of it. Hand your horse to a responsible person and delegate others to control traffic on either side of the accident. Call the emergency services, and send others to catch any loose horses while you attend to and apply first aid to any injured humans and horses. Record the accident details in the incident/accident report book, and notify the insurance company if necessary.

ROLLING

Horses will sometimes roll when they find themselves on an unfamiliar surface, especially if it is soft and inviting, such as wood chippings or sand, when in water, or when they are hot and sweaty.

Pawing at the ground with a forefoot is often a preliminary to rolling, sometimes accompanied by sniffing at the surface. This is followed by the horse buckling at the knees as it goes down (horses lie down front end first), and by the time this stage is reached, if the horse is being ridden it's usually too late to do much about it other than to get off quickly (*see* page 143, Horse Falls). Ideally try to prevent the problem in the first place by being alert to your horse's body language and any indication that he might roll. At the first sign, send him briskly forward, maintaining a positive rein contact to prevent him lowering his head, and keep him moving.

If you can't stop it happening, dismount on the side towards which his shoulder is lowering. Move towards the head so you are out of the

Pawing may be a sign that your horse is about to roll. (Courtesy RAD Photographic)

way of his hooves, and try to keep hold of the reins, if you can do so safely, so they don't get tangled round his feet.

When he has finished rolling, encourage him to get back to his feet, and check him over for any injuries. Rolling is also a symptom of colic, so look for any other indications and if you think this might be the case, seek veterinary assistance: this is potentially an emergency.

Rolling with the saddle on isn't good for either the horse's back or the saddle. If it does occur, ask your saddler to take a look at it, because even though it may look fine, there may be damage to the internal structures. Check your horse's back for signs of tenderness, and consult a vet if necessary.

SEPARATION ANXIETY

Horses are herd animals by nature and may be reluctant to leave their field companions, especially if they are young, inexperienced or lacking in confidence. When asked to go out on their own they may call to the companion left behind, will tend to lack concentration, and pay limited attention to the rider. They will often exhibit a 'high alert' posture, with a high head carriage, shortened, choppy and irregular steps and stiffly pricked ears: the muscles will feel hard, tense and unresponsive. In some cases the horse may begin to relax as the ride progresses, but others will remain in a state of considerable anxiety, and may even attempt to spin round

TTEAM Promise Wrap

Using a TTEAM promise wrap – a 4in elasticated exercise bandage attached to the girth straps on each side and passed around the quarters – improves engagement from behind and can have a calming effect on horses nervous of noises or movement behind them. The bandage should have plenty of stretch left in it so it doesn't slip up or down and maintains a constant contact with the body. Your horse may be used to a fillet string or leg straps on rugs, but a wrap gives a very different feel, so ask someone competent to help you introduce it in small, easy stages on the ground before you try it mounted.

- Tie one end of the bandage to the off-side rear girth strap of the saddle, using a quick release knot.
- Bring the other end of the bandage around the quarters, lifting the tail over the top. Keep hold of the end while your helper leads the horse forwards a short distance: stay on the same side, and level with the horse's sides rather than his quarters, just in case he kicks out. If he moves off rather briskly, hold the bandage more loosely until he is comfortable with the feel.
- Your helper should stay up by the horse's head, as it is easier to control him from there than by the shoulder. Halt and walk forwards again several times.
- If your horse is relaxed about the bandage, tie the other end on to the near-side rear girth strap, using a quick release knot. Join two bandages together if one isn't long enough. The bandage should lie just below the point of the buttocks, and be a snug but not tight fit.
- Ask the horse to walk and halt again several times, and if all is still well, try trotting a couple of times, too.
- If he is unperturbed by this, progress to riding him in it: walk and halt a few times, first with your helper leading, then going solo. If your horse reacts badly at any point to the feel of the wrap or is very concerned, he may have a physical problem which needs attention, so ask your vet to check him over.

Promise Wrap. (Bob Atkins, courtesy Horse & Rider *magazine)*

and return home, or will stop and refuse to move forwards (*see also* page 153, Napping).

Resolving the problem is most likely to be successful if broken down into easy stages, progressing as the horse's self-confidence and trust in the rider develops. Begin by working in a safe enclosed area with other horses, so that your horse feels secure as his companions are present, but begins to learn to focus on his rider. Use school movements and groundwork exercises to help engage his attention: confidence training (*see* page 87, Confidence Training) will also be of benefit.

When hacking out, go with one of his field companions, but don't just follow behind. Where it is safe to do so, ride up alongside each other, and when your horse is settled the other can gradually slow down so that yours draws ahead. To start with this may be only a matter of a few feet, and only for a short while, but as your horse realizes his friend is still there and nothing terrible has happened to him, you should gradually be able to move further ahead for a greater distance, and to remain there for increasingly longer periods of time.

As he becomes less concerned you can vary things by 'leap-frogging' – taking it in turns to overtake each other where it is safe to do so, the horse being overtaken remaining in walk while the other jog trots past. Practise this in the school first so it is already a familiar exercise before trying it out hacking.

When your horse is happy to remain in the lead at a distance of at least fifty feet, and only at a point on your ride when you are very close to home, your escort can gradually slow down as before and then discreetly peel off to take a different route home, so you complete the last section on your own. This may be only a matter of a few hundred yards, but little by little you will be able to build on these small successes: be careful not to try and progress faster than your horse's confidence can cope with. Using TTEAM

TTouches can be helpful in building a bond of mutual trust between you, as well as in lowering stress levels before you set out and on your return. You may also find the Promise Wrap and some of the suggestions on page 16, Hacking Nerves, worth trying.

SHYING AND SPOOKING

Despite many thousands of years of domestication, the survival instinct to run away from anything perceived as threatening remains strongly developed in the horse. There may be warning signs, such as stiffly pricked ears, high head carriage, tense muscles, slowing and elevated steps, rapid breathing and maybe snorting as he prepares for flight – or a spook may come out of nowhere, taking you completely by surprise. Your horse may jump sideways, try to rush past the object of his fear keeping as much distance as possible between himself and it, refuse to go forwards at all (*see also* page 153, Napping) or try to spin round and run off in the opposite direction.

With patience it is possible to reduce this behaviour. First eliminate any possible physical problems, including saddle and bridle fit, physical discomfort from teeth, back or other issues, and eyesight. Poor hearing can also be a contributory cause – he is more likely to be spooked by something he didn't hear approaching – and inappropriate feeding and insufficient turnout can also lead to spooking due to excess energy levels.

A horse that trusts his rider is less likely to spook, and TTEAM work can be invaluable in developing this trust and teaching confidence, self control and the ability to think problems through rather than reacting reflexively.

It can help you relax, too: when riding this sort of horse, the tendency is to shorten the reins and clamp your legs on, which sends all the wrong messages and can inadvertently trigger spooky behaviour. Using the TTEAM Balance Rein (*see* page 138) can help you keep a more relaxed contact; it also encourages your horse to lower his head and neck, which reduces reactive responses. And of course, it will also act as an emergency grab handle!

A number of TTEAM exercises can be used to help your horse learn to stay calm in situations he finds alarming, including Sliding Saddlecloth (*see* page 144), stroking over the whole of his body with a wand (*see* page 163), Promise Wrap (*see* page 158) and working over different surfaces (*see* page 87, Confidence Training). As there simply isn't room to include all of the work which can be of benefit, you may find it helpful to contact a TTEAM practitioner (*see* page 170, Further Information). You may also find some of the suggestions on pages 16–21, Hacking Nerves worth pursuing.

Passing Spooky Objects

When passing something your horse thinks is scary, allow him time to assess the object, using your voice to reassure and encourage him. If on the road, wait for a lull in traffic, or ask vehicles to wait so your horse can pass at a distance he feels safe at. The less of a drama you make about it the more confident he will be next time a similar situation arises. Don't stare at the object yourself, but look ahead and visualize your horse going quietly past it.

If you have to dismount to lead your horse past, make sure you take the reins over his head and hold them in both hands. Stay up by his head so you have better control over his speed in case he tries to rush, and position yourself between him and the spooky object. As when riding, allow him to pass at a distance he feels safe at.

The wrong way to pass a spooky object.

VISION

Horses are very sensitive to movement – not just people, animals, or a plastic bag blowing around, but also shadows moving on the ground as tree branches sway overhead, or the reflection of light off ripples on water. Although they see reasonably well in dim light conditions, their sight adjusts more slowly than ours when moving from bright to shady areas, so they may be spooky or hesitant because they can't see what's ahead properly.

With eyes set towards the side of the head, a horse has fairly good all-round vision. He can use both eyes together, or he can look at his surroundings on both sides, using either eye. This helps explain why you can accustom your horse to passing an object on one rein, but he will still spook at it when passing in the opposite direction – he is seeing it for the first time with the other eye. Studies also indicate that horses seem to have a left eye preference, and will try to view frightening objects with that eye.

The right way to pass a spooky object: flex him slightly in the opposite direction, asking for a shoulder-in position if you both know how to do this. This enables you to keep better control, and when on roads, will stop the quarters from swinging out into passing traffic.

SLIPPING SADDLE

Poor conformation, poor saddle fit, and an insufficiently tight girth can all cause your saddle to slip, and the problem will be

To check the girth when mounted, place both reins into your right hand, maintaining a contact with your horse's mouth. With your left hand, reach down in front of your left leg: you should be able to slip three fingers comfortably between the girth and your horse's sides.

To tighten the girth while mounted, place both reins in your right hand, and swing your left leg forward over the front of the saddle flap, keeping your foot in the stirrup. This stops the stirrup iron from swinging and bumping against your horse's sides, which could make him fidget. It also enables you to quickly be back in control with both feet securely in the stirrups if anything unexpected happens. Lift the saddle flap with your left hand, and pull up each girth strap in turn, using your index finger to guide the buckle tongue into the hole. If your saddle has long girth straps with a short girth, keep both feet in the stirrups as before, but lean forwards and reach down in front of your leg to tighten it while mounted.

aggravated if the rider is crooked, the horse overweight, and when tackling steep up- or downhill inclines. It can cause discomfort, lead to injury and in some cases may actually scare the horse.

If you feel the saddle begin to slip, slow the horse to a walk or halt and dismount, keeping hold of the reins as you do so. Reassure the

horse if he is anxious, and run the stirrup irons up the leathers so they don't swing around. Don't try and push the saddle back into place. Undo the girth, support the saddle to stop it falling to the ground, and carefully reposition it before girthing up again.

Check the girth is tight enough before and after mounting, and again after riding for ten to fifteen minutes. If the saddle slips regularly, ask your saddler to check the fit and see what can be done to minimize the problem. (*See also* page 31, Saddlery, and page 21, Young Riders.)

STUMBLING

If your horse stumbles, take a handful of mane or hold the neckstrap rather than pulling on the reins to keep yourself secure; your horse may need free movement of his neck to regain his balance. Should your horse stumble so badly that he actually begins to go down, dismount immediately (*see* page 145, Emergency Dismount).

Stumbling may be due to a momentary loss of concentration and balance while working on uneven, tussocky or rutted ground; horses which work on the forehand or lack experience may be more prone to stumble, and will benefit from schooling and work over ground poles to help remedy this. Using a TTEAM Balance Rein will also be beneficial (*see* page 138).

If stumbling is due to fatigue, dismount and lead your horse home as this will be safer for both of you, and aim to either work within his physical ability in the future, or increase his level of fitness so he is able to cope with the intensity and duration of the riding you want to do (*see* page 13, Fit for Purpose).

Stumbling can also be due to physical problems including lameness, arthritic conditions, overlong feet in need of shoeing, or back problems (*see* page 37, Hoofcare, and page 147, Lame Horse): ask your vet to advise.

TTEAM Single Pole Exercise

This pole exercise looks simple but requires a huge amount of co-ordination, and is excellent for teaching better motor skills. It will also improve balance and self control, develop concentration (often the most difficult 'skill' to teach), reduce one-sided tendencies and generally help make your horse more manoeuvrable. You can do this exercise while mounted, when it's also a great way of improving your own sense of 'feel' and the precision and subtlety of your communication with your horse, but it's a good idea to start off by teaching it in hand. As well as being easier for your horse to learn without someone on his back, it gives you the chance to observe what he's doing, and makes it easier for you to assist him.

Don't rush your horse or reprimand him if he seems clumsy or slow to respond at first: just like you when learning a new task, it may take him a little longer than usual to organize himself. Be patient and allow him time to work out what to do and how to do it.

Spread the steps shown here over several sessions, progressing to the next only when your horse has successfully completed the previous one; at the start of each new session repeat the earlier steps as a confidence-giving reminder. Move the pole to different places in your working area and approach it from opposite directions, too: you may be surprised at how much this can change things.

Don't repeat the exercise to the point where you or your horse becomes bored or tired, as this is when mistakes happen, which can sap his confidence. Just ten minutes of this work requires a very high level of intense concentration and physical co-ordination: better to stop early, on a good effort.

A long schooling whip or 'wand' is used like an extension of your arm, and enables you to touch areas of your horse's body you couldn't otherwise easily or safely reach in order to provide information about his body and to guide or cue actions. Practise using it on another person and then on your horse before trying it during the pole exercise. Hold it like a sword, but keeping your grip relaxed so you can use it with delicacy and precision. Use a downward stroking movement on the underside of the neck and the front of the chest, and then work your way down the front, then the back of the forelegs, along the back, ribcage and belly, then over quarters and down the hind legs. Keep the contact gentle but firm rather than light and tickly, and use steady, smooth movements. If the horse is nervous, take time introducing this, reversing the wand in your hand initially so just a short length of the handle protrudes, and stroking him down the underside of his neck and front of the chest with it. The wand can also help you encourage your horse to slow or stop by touching him with it on the front of his chest or on the point of shoulder on the side furthest from you. (Bob Atkins, courtesy Horse & Rider *magazine)*

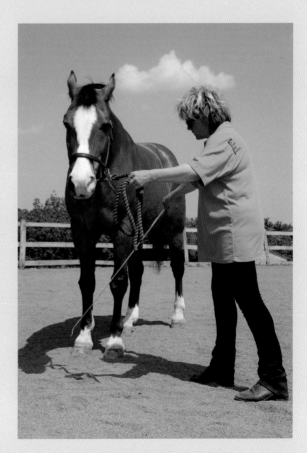

You will need the following equipment:

- Headcollar: A close but not tight fit so it won't slip about on your horse's head.
- Leadrein: Attach the leadrein to the side ring on the noseband rather than under the jaw, as this lessens poll pressure and allows you to give lighter signals.
- A pole 10–12ft in length.
- A 'wand': a 4ft long, stiff but slightly flexible schooling whip.

The Exercise
- Start by walking over the pole, watching closely to see exactly what your horse does. Does he always step over it with the same foot going over first? Like us, horses have definite left/right preferences, and if this is the case, to what extent will he adjust his stride in order to always put the favoured foot over first: does he shuffle in an extra little short step, or take a longer but unbalanced and lurching step? Also note whether he moves over it straight or slightly crookedly, and if this is the same on both reins, or more marked when going in a certain direction.
- Does he clear the pole with all four feet, or rap it with any of them – and is it always the same feet? Does he lift all his feet the same height? Does his headcarriage change in any way? The more you observe your horse in action, the more you will learn about him and any difficulties he has, which will make it easier for you to help him.
- When you have done this a couple of times, ask your horse to halt just in front of the pole. Give yourself plenty of space to do this as he may anticipate continuing straight over it as before.
- Now ask him to move forwards a step or two and then halt again, so he is standing over the pole with his forelegs on one side

Begin the exercise by asking your horse to halt with front feet on one side of a pole and back feet on the other. (Bob Atkins, courtesy Horse & Rider *magazine)*

Straddling the pole with the front feet requires good balance and co-ordination.
(Bob Atkins, courtesy Horse & Rider *magazine)*

and back legs on the other. It may take a few attempts to get it right, so be patient! Praise your horse when he does, and when you ask him to walk on again, encourage him to do so slowly. This is good for improving balance as well as increasing awareness of rear foot placement.

- The next step is to halt your horse again just in front of the pole. This time ask him to move just one foreleg forwards so he is straddling the pole with a front foot on each side. This degree of precision and control can be very difficult for some horses, and to be successful he'll need to be in a good balance and to distribute the weight appropriately between the front feet. Horses that are tight through their shoulders or have a high headcarriage will find it hard to stretch through the shoulder, and those that are on their forehand may struggle to achieve the delicacy of movement necessary.

If your horse finds it hard, be patient: as he learns how to organize his body better to meet the challenges of the exercise he will begin to find it easier. You will start to notice that as a result his posture, suppleness, balance, and freedom and length of stride all improve.

- Your horse may only be able to maintain the straddling posture momentarily at first, and will then need to move forwards again: don't check or reprimand him if this happens. With practice he will gradually be able to pause in this position for a little longer. Ask him to step forwards with his other foot so he is standing over the pole with both front legs on one side and back legs on the other as before, pause for a moment, praise him, and then move him forwards once again.

- If your horse tends always to place the same forefoot over the pole, once he is completing

ABOVE: Ask your horse to straddle the pole with either forefoot. (Bob Atkins, courtesy Horse & Rider magazine)

BELOW: Straddling a pole with the back feet is more challenging. (Bob Atkins, courtesy Horse & Rider magazine)

Teaching your horse to move back step-by-step as well as forwards can be helpful if you need to manoeuvre him in a tight space or with precision. (Bob Atkins, courtesy **Horse & Rider** *magazine)*

the two preceding steps confidently you can start reducing this one-sided bias by asking him to step over it with the less favoured leg first instead. Use the wand to stroke down the length of the foreleg you want him to move, and if he still seems a little stuck, stroke again and as you reach his foot, reverse the wand and tap gently on the hoof wall with the hard button on the handle. Again, be patient – this may be challenging stuff for your horse: if he appears to fidget or hesitate he's not being naughty or resistant, but trying to work out how to do something he's not quite sure about.

- Once you've mastered straddling a pole with either forefoot moving first, you can teach your horse to do the same with his hind feet in much the same way. This can be considerably more difficult, and you must have successfully completed the front leg work first.
- Finally, try varying the exercise by stepping

over the pole as before, pausing, and then asking your horse to lift a foot and this time to move it back over the pole. This can be a wonderful co-ordination and balance exercise, and can be invaluable if you need to manoeuvre your horse with precision or in a confined space.

Other Polework

Other ways in which you can use poles include the following:

- Walking over one or more poles, but crossing them at an angle.
- Set up several poles with varying rather than uniformly predictable distances between them.
- Place poles at angles to each other.
- Raise one end of one or more poles to give a variety of heights.
- Raise the opposite ends of alternate poles.

TONGUE OVER BIT

If your horse gets his tongue over the bit, the discomfort can cause him to panic: he may throw his head around – sometimes quite violently – and you will certainly notice the sudden lack of control. Sometimes you may spot his tongue protruding from the side of his mouth.

Slow to a walk or halt as best you are able, then lengthen the reins to minimize his discomfort and also the possibility that it might cause him to rear or run backwards. Dismount immediately (*see* page 145, Emergency Dismount), leaving the reins around his neck rather than taking them over his head.

Unbuckle the bridle cheekpiece on one side, and lower the bit sufficiently that he can draw his tongue back underneath it again, then refasten it at the correct height. Do this carefully, as he may throw his head around and could catch you in the face.

As soon as you can, inspect his mouth for cuts and bruising, and take action to try and prevent this situation recurring: it is most likely to happen with a jointed bit which is hanging too low in the mouth, or is too wide. Even so, getting the tongue displaced over the bit can still sometimes happen, and some horses become expert at it. If it keeps occurring, get his teeth checked and investigate other bitting

Approach cattlegrids with great care.

alternatives – or even whether he might be happier in a bitless bridle of some kind.

TRAPPED IN A CATTLEGRID

Thankfully this isn't a common occurrence; such accidents generally occur either as a result of a horse straying, or the horse running away after the rider has fallen off. If your horse does become trapped in a grid you will not be able to free him by yourself. Keep him as calm and quiet as possible so he doesn't injure himself further, and contact your vet and the emergency services immediately. (*See also* page 82, Cattlegrids.)

WOUNDS

If your horse sustains a minor cut while out on a ride it will be fine until you reach home and can clean and treat it (*see* page 108, Post-ride Checks). More serious wounds involving damage to an artery or vein may bleed profusely, and require immediate emergency first aid as well as urgent veterinary attention.

Place a sterile non-stick dressing directly over the wound, and place a pad of gamgee over the top of this, holding it firmly in place with a bandage. If the bleeding continues and soaks through the dressing, don't remove it but add additional layers of padding and bandage, and increase the pressure until the bleeding stops. If you don't have everything you need to hand, then improvise with whatever you do have, such as items of clothing. If you have nothing with which to hold a pressure pad in place, or if the injury is in an area you can't bandage, hold it there as tightly as possible.

If there are multiple wounds, deal with the most serious first. Try to be reassuring, keeping your horse calm and as still as possible: excitement and movement will make the heart beat faster and increase the rate of bleeding. Watch for signs of shock (*see* panel below)

SHOCK

Shock is a serious medical condition which can be life threatening. Causes may be obvious – such as external wounds – but may also be due to unseen internal injury. Signs of shock include the following:

- Shaking or shivering.
- Rapid breathing.
- Weak pulse.
- Very pale mucous membranes, or with a blue-grey tinge.
- Cold extremities – the ears are always a good guide.

Send for urgent veterinary attention. Place a rug or jacket or any other clothing available over the horse's loins to help keep him warm – even if the weather is warm. While waiting for the vet, doing TTEAM ear work (*see* page 19, Hacking Nerves) can help keep your horse from going into shock: as you reach the tip of the ear rub it between forefinger and thumb to activate the shock acupoint located there. Keep repeating, working one ear at a time rather than both together, as this usually seems to be more effective.

Further Information

USEFUL CONTACTS

The Access Company
www.theaccesscompany.co.uk

Alexander Technique
www.stat.org.uk

Association of British Riding Schools (ABRS)
www.abrs-info.org

Association of Chartered Physiotherapists in
Animal Therapy (ACPAT)
www.acpat.org

Association of Irish Riding Establishments
www.aire.ie

Association of Pet Behaviour Counsellors
www.apbc.org.uk

Australian Trail Horse Riders' Association
www.athra.com.au

Bach Flower essences
www.bachcentre.com

Back Country Horsemen of America
www.backcountryhorse.com

Barefoot riding
www.thenaturalhoof.co.uk

Bridleways
www.bridleways.co.uk

British Association of Homoeopathic Veterinary
Surgeons
www.bahvs.com

British Equestrian Trade Association (BETA)
www.beta-uk.org

British Equine Veterinary Association
www.beva.org.uk

British Horse Society
www.bhs.org.uk

British Horse Society Ireland
www.bhsireland.com

British Horse Society Scotland
www.bhsscotland.org.uk

British Red Cross
www.redcross.org.uk

Byways and Bridleways Trust
www.bbtrust.org.uk

Clicker training
www.theclickercenter.com

Countryside Access and Activities Network
Northern Ireland
www.countrysiderecreation.com

Countryside Council for Wales
www.ccw.gov.uk

Endurance GB
www.endurancegb.co.uk

Equine Mapping and Geographical Information
Network (EMAGIN)
www.emagin.org

Equine Ramblers
www.equineramblers.co.uk

Farriers Registration Council
www.farrier-reg.gov.uk

Forestry Commission
www.forestry.gov.uk

Fun rides
www.ridingdiary.co.uk

Google maps
www.maps.google.co.uk

Google Earth
www.earth.google.com

Harvey maps
www.harveymaps.co.uk

Health and Safety Executive (HSE)
www.hse.gov.uk

Highway Code
www.direct.gov.uk/highwaycode

Horse & Rider magazine
www.horseandrideruk.com

Institute of Public Rights of Way and Access
Management
www.iprow.co.uk

Ireland Forest Service
www.coilteoutdoors.ie

Irish Long Distance Riding Association (ILDRA)
www.enduranceridingireland.com

The Longriders Guild
www.thelongridersguild.com

The Mark Davies Injured Riders Fund
www.mdirf.co.uk

McTimoney Chiropractic Association
www.mctimoneychiropractic.org
and
www.mctimoney-animal.org.uk

Ministry of Defence
MoD Freephone Helpline: Tel 0800 51 55 44
Complaints and Enquiries Unit: Tel 0207 218
6020
www.mod.uk

Multi Agency Geographic Information for the
Countryside (MAGIC)
www.magic.gov.uk

National Bridle Route Network
www.ride-uk.org.uk

Natural England
www.naturalengland.org.uk

Open Spaces Society
www.oss.org.uk

Ordnance Survey
www.ordnancesurvey.co.uk

Organisation of Horsebox and Trailer Owners
www.ohto.co.uk

Pony Club
www.pcuk.org

Pony magazine
www.ponymag.com

Royal College of Veterinary Surgeons
www.rcvs.org.uk

Scottish Border rides
www.rideborders.com

Scottish Endurance Riding Club
www.scottishendurance.com

Scottish Natural Heritage
www.snh.gov.uk

Scottish Outdoor Access Code
www.outdooraccess-scotland.com

Scottish Rights of Way and Access Society
www.scotways.com

Stanford's map shop
www.stanfords.co.uk

State Forest Service (Northern Ireland)
www.forestserviceni.gov.uk

Streetmap
www.streetmap.co.uk

St. John Ambulance
www.sja.org.uk

St. Andrews First Aid
www.firstaid.org.uk

Ticks
www.lymediseaseaction.org.uk

Tide Times
www.easytide.co.uk

Toll Rides (Off-Road) Trust (TROT)
www.tollrides.org.uk

Towing Horse Trailers
www.towinghorsetrailers.co.uk

Trec
www.bhs.org.uk
and
www.trec-uk.com

Trekking and Riding Society of Scotland
www.ridinginscotland.com

TTEAM UK
www.ttouchtteam.co.uk

UK Chasers
www.ukchasers.com

Water crossings
www.wetroads.co.uk

Weather
www.xcweather.co.uk

Further Reading

Belsey, Valerie *Discovering Green Lanes*

Bush, Karen and Marczak, Julian *101 Riding Exercises*

First Aid Manual: The Authorised Manual of St John Ambulance, St Andrews Ambulance Association and the British Red Cross

Fisher, Sarah *Know Your Horse Inside Out*

Harris, Charles *Fundamentals of Riding*

Kurland, Alexandra *Clicker Training for your Horse*

Marczak, Julian and Bush, Karen *The Principles of Teaching Riding*

McGreevy, Paul *Why Does my Horse?*

Paisley, Professor R. *Access Rights and Rights of Way: A guide to the law in Scotland* (Scotways)

Riddall, John and Trevelyan, John *Rights of Way: A guide to Law and Practice* (4th edition)

Sutton, Amanda *The Injured Horse*

Tellington-Jones, Linda *The Ultimate Horse Behaviour and Training Book*

Index